Anne Murray

The Story So Far

Anne Murray

The Story So Far

David Livingstone

A Madison Press Book

COLLIER BOOKS
A Division of Macmillan Publishing Co., Inc.
New York

Published in the United States of America by
Collier Books,
A Division of Macmillan Publishing Co., Inc.,
866 Third Avenue,
New York, N.Y. 10022.

Library of Congress Catalog Card Number: 81-13729

First American Edition 1981.

ISBN 0-02-004520-4

Published in Canada by
Prentice-Hall Canada Inc.

Canadian Cataloguing in Publication Data

Livingstone, David.
Anne Murray: the story so far

ISBN 0-13-037697-3

1. Murray, Anne. 2. Singers — Canada — Biography.
I. Title.
ML420.M87L58   784.5′0092′4   C81-094691-2

Produced by
Madison Press Books,
149 Lowther Avenue,
Toronto, Ontario,
Canada M5R 3M5.

Editor: Shelley Tanaka
Designer: Keith Abraham
Picture researcher: Carroll Gair
Typesetting by Trigraph Inc., Toronto
Film separations by Colourgraph Inc., Toronto
Printed in Canada by Arthurs-Jones Lithographing Ltd., Toronto

Acknowledgments

The publishers gratefully acknowledge the following sources for permission to use photographs in this book.

Black-and-white photographs: CBS: pages 59, 79, 80. CP Photo: pages 13, 46, 68 (top), 82. CTV: page 88. Canadian Broadcasting Corporation: 34, 35, 37, 38, 39, 42 (top), 47 (top), 48. Canadian Imperial Bank of Commerce/McKim Advertising: page 113. Capitol Records, EMI of Canada Limited: pages 53 (Photographer: Richard Creamer), 55 (Photographer: John Wyckoff), 72 (Photographer: John Wyckoff), 76, 88, 127, 128 (bottom). Bruce Cole, Plum Studios Inc.: page 58. Croton Studios, Vancouver, page 20. Ken Elliot: page 126. *Globe and Mail*, page 18. Sherman Hines Photographic Limited: page 120. Don Jacobsen: pages 12, 107. Bill Langstroth: pages 8, 10, 14, 19, 44, 47 (bottom), 50, 51, 52, 56, 64, 67, 69, 70, 73, 82, 84, 92, 94, 95, 96, 97, 98, 102, 105, 106, 108, 109, 110, 114, 115, 117, 130. David Livingstone: pages 30, 129. Donna-Lynn McCallum: pages 17, 54, 83. Brian D. McLaughlin: page 77. Lorne Pridham Studio of Photography, Saint John: page 87. Robert C. Ragsdale, page 31. © 1981 Ebet Roberts: pages 15 (top), 78, 104 (right), 123. John Rowlands: pages 15 (bottom), 16, 49, 60, 61 (top), 74, 75, 90, 93, 101, 128. Toronto *Star*: pages 32, 91, 122. Toshiba EMI: page 66. Wamboldt-Waterfield Photography: pages 36, 41, 42 (bottom), 68 (bottom), 86 (right), 89. Jim Welander: page 125. Harold Whyte: page 112. Natalie Wojcinski: pages 116, 124.

Colour photographs (*in order of appearance*): Barry Ashley: 4. Canadian Broadcasting Corporation: 3. Don Jacobsen: 9, 10. Bill Langstroth: 2, 5, 6, 7, 8. Gord Marci: 1, 11.
Front cover: Gord Marci. Back cover: Bill Langstroth

Although every effort has been made to insure that permissions for all material were obtained, those sources not formally acknowledged here will be included in all future editions of this book.

The publisher wishes especially to thank Bill Langstroth for his enthusiastic help and co-operation with this project.

Contents

Foreword

THIS book was prepared with the generous co-operation of Anne Murray and Leonard Rambeau, president of Balmur Limited. Bill Langstroth was kind to entrust many boxes of slides. It was also my pleasure to take the bus from Moncton, New Brunswick to Springhill, Nova Scotia and to be met by Mrs. Marion Murray, Anne's mother. Her hospitality was an encouragement.

I also drew confidence from Anne herself. Besides being faithful to the facts, I hope what I have done is true to her private, dignified and strangely elusive nature.

David Livingstone

one

Star on the Rise

THERE'S no business like show business. You don't have to go to Detroit to hear people say "right on" to that statement. But on September 1, 1980, the Michigan State Fair was gloriously exemplary of that enduring truth.

It's 3:30 in the afternoon. Dressed in peach-colored silk and chiffon, Anne Murray has just completed a matinee, the first of two performances that day, and is making her way off the outdoor stage. An early-morning storm has turned the grounds into mud. Anne is wearing slingback sandals with medium heels that she finds comfortable on stage; they also make it easier for her to walk the planks that lead to her trailer backstage. She stops to receive a compliment from a security guard who enjoyed the show, and then steps inside, where she is going to to be interviewed by a Canadian crew from nearby Windsor. After a moment, she reappears, poking her head out the door to see if anybody's got a cigarette. At home, she keeps her pack of cigarettes in the kitchen cupboard and can go for weeks without them. But, that's the biz. Sometimes there's mud and sometimes you just have to have a smoke.

Ten years after her first international smash hit, "Snowbird," there's no question that Anne Murray is in show business. She's had a long list of singles, placing on both pop and country charts. She has become a favorite in such far reaches of the globe as Australia, New Zealand, Japan and Hong Kong. There have been gold and platinum albums in the United States, and even more in her native land, Canada, where in the

Anne poses in front of only a few gold records that are the solid signals of her success. However, she is not so carried away by any of it that she can't matter-of-factly fold her arms and grin.

summer of 1980 she was named female recording artist of the decade. Tributes include three Grammys, for "Love Song" in 1975, "You Needed Me" in 1978, and "Could I Have This Dance?" in 1980.

But still, besides her unique contralto voice, what distinguishes Anne Murray from other female singers who have had hits and won prizes is some quality of character that is the opposite of show business. Back in the late sixties, when Anne first turned professional, you might have said she was "real"—not plastic. When Anne played Las Vegas in 1979, foremost in her mind on opening night was making sure that there were enough diapers for her infant daughter. Perhaps that says it all.

It was quite clear that day at the fair in Detroit that there's show business and there's show business. Anne seems especially down-to-earth compared to some of the types who wait outside her trailer, including a young woman decorated in banners proclaiming her to be both Junior Miss Michigan and Michigan's Junior Talent. Maybe ten or eleven, wearing a tiara

March 10, 1981: Anne usually avoids ambassadorial airs, presenting herself as herself and not making hay of the fact that she happens to be one of the most famous Canadians in history. But when the Canadian government pulled out all the stops to welcome President Reagan on his first official visit to the country, Anne featured prominently among the best talents the country has to display. Following an entertainment gala at the National Arts Centre in Ottawa, Anne meets with the President and his wife Nancy.

and mauve shadow over bright eyes, she carefully explains that although she won the talent competition with her Tahitian dancing, she is branching out into singing. Just as thoroughly she also explains that she had the option of meeting Ronald Reagan, campaigning somewhere on the grounds, but chose instead to meet Miss Murray.

She does, but first in line is a Reagan emissary waiting to find out if Anne would like to drop over and say a public hello to the presidential candidate. Once a director of entertainment at Disneyland, the man, to borrow his lingo, is doing "advance work" for Reagan, looking out for "the right television situations," that kind of thing. Leonard Rambeau, Anne's manager, informs him that Anne will take a pass. A professional associate of Anne's since 1969, Rambeau is a walking compendium of Murrayana, but one thing he doesn't know about her is how she votes. In general, she doesn't mix her politics with show business. Her decision not to meet Reagan has nothing to do with what she thinks of him. She just doesn't want to appear to be endorsing anybody.

To the degree that she must be careful about such things, Anne Murray is image-conscious. No fool, she knows she's in show business. More important, she knows when the show is over. Between performances at the Michigan State Fair, she changes out of her silk and chiffon into the plaid shirt and white coveralls she was wearing when she arrived. She bought the coveralls in Monte Carlo, but as glamorous as shopping in Monte might sound, there's not much about life on the road

In Monte Carlo in the summer of 1980, Anne taped a guest appearance on a Kris Kristofferson special. "It's the first time that I have ever been able to look in someone's eyes and sing and really, honestly get that look back."

High spirits reign after Anne's sold-out concert at New York's Radio City Music Hall in November 1980. Anne shares a laugh with Billie Jean King and Ron Duguay, Canadian-born star attraction of the New York Rangers hockey team, otherwise known for his appearances in ads for Oo-la-la jeans. Before Anne Murray, hockey stars and furs were Canada's best-known exports.

Anne says she gets tongue-tied when she visits backstage. But following Helen Reddy's performance at the Canadian National Exhibition in 1977, Anne dropped by.

that she enjoys, not even shopping. Across the way, in another trailer, the eight musicians who travel with her are cutting up on their own. In response to the obvious question about why she isn't cutting loose with the band, she says, "I think a working relationship is better when you stay removed from it."

Eminently level-headed, Anne Murray is not a star in the usual mold. Foregoing glamour for good sense, she is brazenly normal. To some people, Anne represents a homespun style thought to be somehow typical of Canada, land of the silver birch, home of the beaver. But, while she has attained a scale of international prominence most Canadian entertainers traditionally have not dreamt of, Anne declines the burden of being a national symbol. "My biggest problem at one time was the introduction I would always get, 'Canadian' this, 'Canadian' that. I got a little sick of it. What has that got to do with anything? Is that a qualifying statement, because I'm Canadian, dada dada dada . . . or mean that I should be given special attention or, I don't know, whether they couldn't think of other adjectives."

Opposite. Natural is such a vague word to describe Anne's charm in performance. Look at that face.

Five strikes and you're out?! Anne gives some basic instruction in mathematics to a young fan, after singing the national anthem at the opening game of the Toronto Blue Jays, the city's baseball club, in April 1977.

If there are any environmental factors that might explain her rise to the top, they stem not from Canada but from a particular part of Canada. Anne regards the Maritimes as a "really important part of the world" and, she says, she is making a point to see that her children spend some time there. No matter what Anne says, it's clear from how she says it that she was born in Nova Scotia. And beyond the accents of her speech she bears traces of Nova Scotia in her blood.

Caught off-guard, Anne displays a serious aspect.

Traditionally Anne spends her summer holidays in Nova Scotia. In the summer of 1981 she and Bill bought a three-bedroom winterized cottage with eight acres. Eight "mowed" acres, Anne takes the trouble to point out.

two

Down Home in the Maritimes

MORNA ANNE MURRAY was born at 10:40 in the morning on June 20, 1945. She was born at All Saints' Hospital in Springhill, Nova Scotia, although it's probably enough to say *the* hospital, since in that small mining town there has always been only one. Anne's five brothers—three older, two younger—were all born there, and it was there that her parents first met. Both were natives of places close to and smaller than Springhill. From Tatamagouche, the son of Dr. Dan Murray and Morna Carson, Dr. James Carson Murray was a recent medical graduate and Presbyterian. From Joggins, the daughter of coal miner Arthur Burke and Mary Beliveau, Marion Margaret Burke was a nurse-in-training and Roman Catholic. When they married, neither one's parents came to the wedding. Nevertheless, despite a controversial beginning, their life together was characterized by uncommon bliss and accord.

Anne was raised in the faith of her mother, but her father was also extremely important in shaping her spirit. She thought the world of him, and remembers once being thrown into childish fear and confusion by someone telling her that

Some of Anne's people in a family shot taken not longer after Carson Murray and Marion Burke were married. In front, left to right: Anne's grandfather, Dr. Dan; Uncle Bert and Aunt Ethel; Anne's grandmother. In back, left to right: Anne's mother and father; Anne's mother's sister, Erma; Anne's father's brother, Don, and his wife.

Anne's maternal grandparents, Mr. and Mrs. Arthur Burke, on their forty-fifth wedding anniversary. Anne's mother says, "We weren't the picture-taking family. There had to be an occasion."

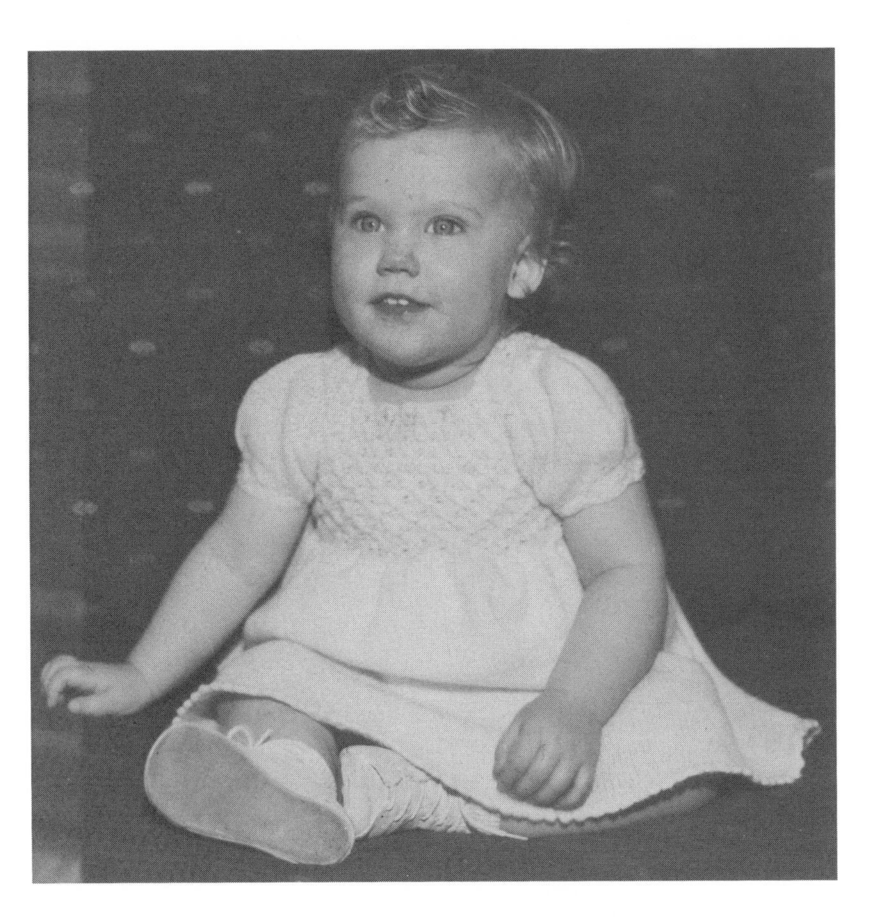

Anne at ten months. "Dawn looks like that."

Anne and her father.

eternal salvation was reserved only for Catholics. "How could anyone say that my father wasn't going to heaven? As far as I was concerned, he was the closest thing to God there was." A man of quiet dedication, who valued a sound mind no less than a sound body, Dr. Carson Murray liked to keep active and was fond of poetry. He ran. He also recited Wordsworth. In the tradition of good country doctors he worked long hours. For recreation, he enjoyed "anything that got him away from people." He went hunting and fishing, although landing the big one was not necessarily the point of the exercise. "He used to take us fishing, and when we finished, we'd always go picking Mayflowers. We never caught any fish, but it wasn't until later that I realized that he didn't take us to the best fishing holes. He took us where the Mayflowers were." It was only after her father died, in early spring 1980, that Anne fully understood his stature in the community. She was still finding out things in the funeral home, learning about feats and favors that Dr. Murray had performed and kept to himself.

Anne's mother knew better the position that went with her husband's profession. Although she had taught grades one to ten for a year when she was sixteen and sometimes worked as a nurse, she was thought of in town as Mrs. Murray, the surgeon's wife. Her own talents were spent privately on family and drew less public notice. Husband gone, children all grown and one of them an international star, Marion Murray is apt to speak rashly of herself as a "non-entity." However, you have only to set foot in her beautifully kept home to appreciate her strength.

Neatly labeled jars on the kitchen counter, home-baked bread, and floors clean enough to eat it off suggest the sound and comfortable upbringing that she provided. Credit for the tidy house belongs in part to Dena, a woman who has been coming in four days a week for more than thirty years, but the gracious, hospitable tone is Marion Murray's separate accomplishment. Coming from a coal miner's home where, Anne says, "they didn't have a lot," Mrs. Murray learned early the importance of taking care of things. She has a gift for practical matters, and it was she who helped Anne with her math homework.

From her father Anne inherited a dimpled chin and a dislike of crowds. The shape of her face and her poise come from her mother. Always, according to Anne, "a snappy dresser," Mrs. Murray has a glamorous streak which has been

Opposite. "It's hard to say how old I was then. I would think probably three or four. I can't imagine a child of two posing like that."

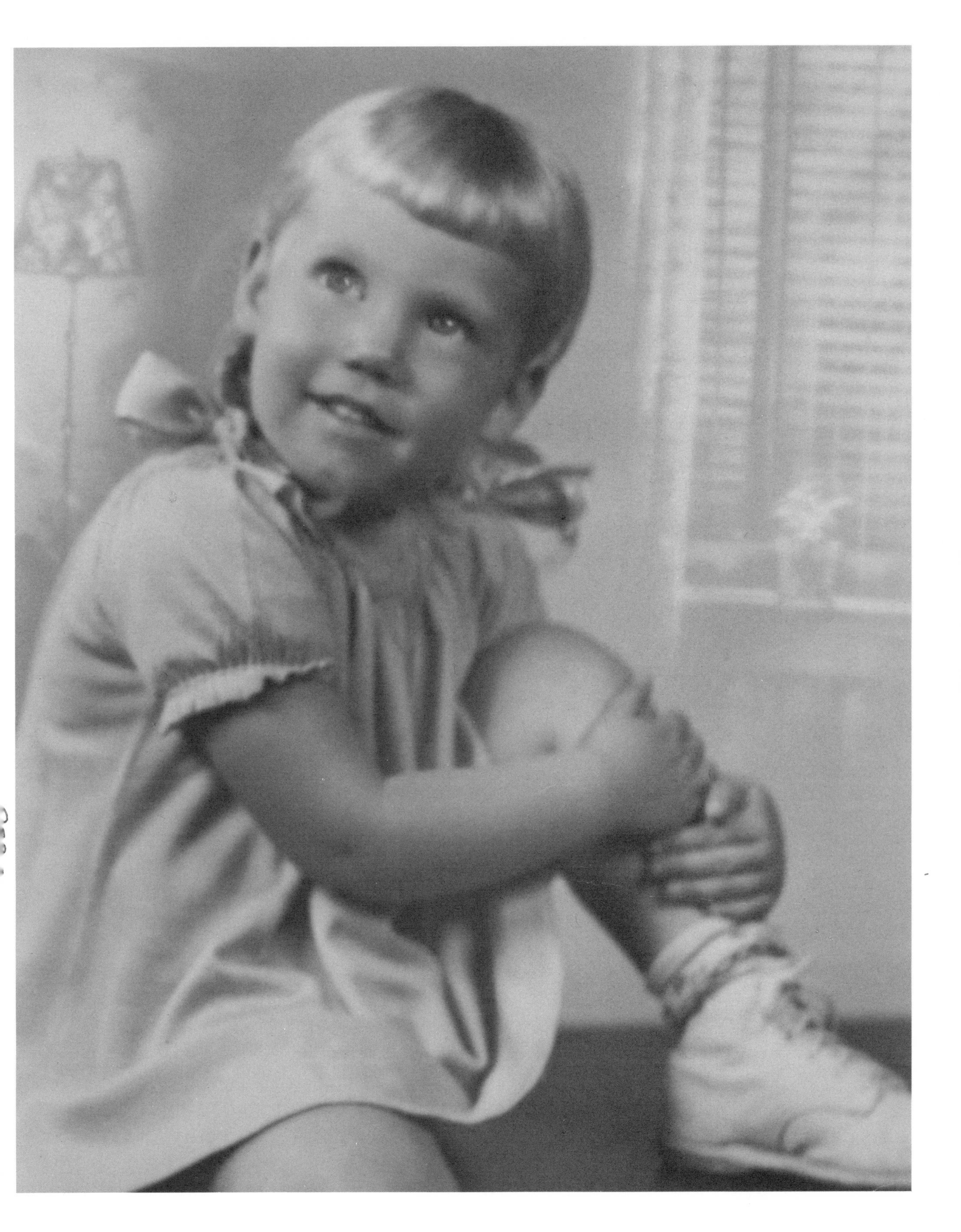

"Mum tried so hard to curl that hair."

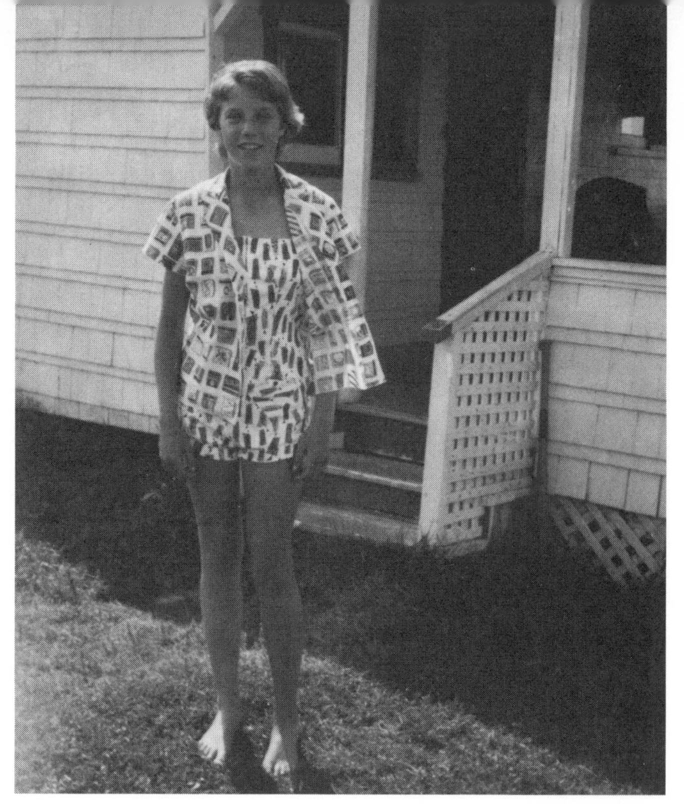

"Great legs, though."

passed on to Anne's brother Bruce. Bruce is the other professional singer in the family. Although so far most familiar as a regular back-up singer with his sister, Bruce has faced with aplomb disparaging remarks about being "the other Murray," and is unabashedly determined to make it on his own merit.

Shy of cameras herself, Mrs. Murray proudly displays photographs of all her family. David is a doctor in Newfoundland. Daniel, a geologist, and Harold, another doctor, live elsewhere in Nova Scotia. Stewart, like all his brothers, graduated from Saint Francis Xavier University in Antigonish, Nova Scotia, but is the only one still living in Springhill. He works as a classification officer at a medium-security prison. All are married and so far there are thirteen grandchildren. As a record to be passed on to Anne's children, Mrs. Murray keeps albums of pictures, press clippings and other mementos of her daughter's career.

While physically Anne finds herself daily growing more like her mother, temperamentally she takes after her placid, unworldly father. Except for keeping herself well-scrubbed, she doesn't like to fuss over her appearance. Mrs. Murray, a regular reader of *Parent's Magazine*, tried thanklessly to instill in her only daughter the little vanities traditionally deemed appropriate for young females. But Anne was more interested in baseball than barrettes.

Carson and Marion Murray were not indulgent parents.

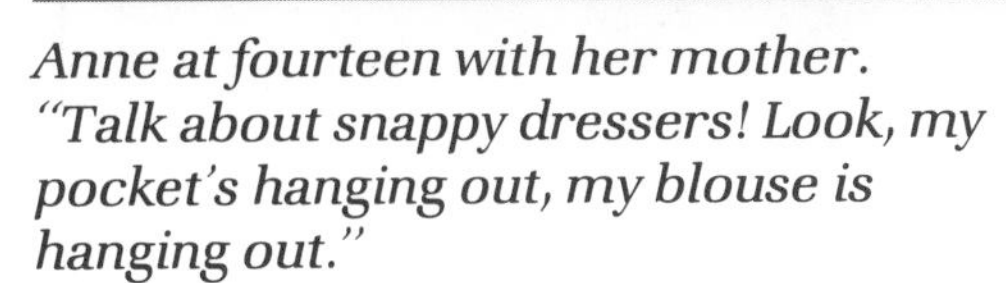

Anne at fourteen with her mother. "Talk about snappy dressers! Look, my pocket's hanging out, my blouse is hanging out."

"Cute, real cute. . . . Oh God, I was so ugly."

They drew boundaries. However, they were not rigid about enforcing them and won their children's respect without resorting to force. Anne's father spanked her once when she was four, "because I wouldn't do something for Mum and when she said, 'I'll get your father,' I said, 'well what do I care?' —he hadn't touched me before. He said, 'would you *please* go downstairs and get the toothpaste?' And I said 'No.' " After that, Anne remembers that all her father had to do was shake his head and "we wouldn't move." Even when she was a typical teenager, thinking that she knew everything and her parents knew nothing, there were no memorable rows. Anne has no recollection of her mother ever telling her that she had to be in by a certain time. In fact, she laughs to recall the many Friday nights her mother may have wished she were out. While she plastered her bedroom with pin-ups of Tony Dow (he played the Beaver's older brother on the *Leave It to Beaver* television series), Anne felt self-conscious with boys. In her teen years, both sports and singing figured more prominently than dates.

Because there were no facilities in her high school, Anne missed out on gym classes. Musically, however, she was formally trained. She studied piano and, when she was fifteen, started taking voice lessons. She was also a member of an

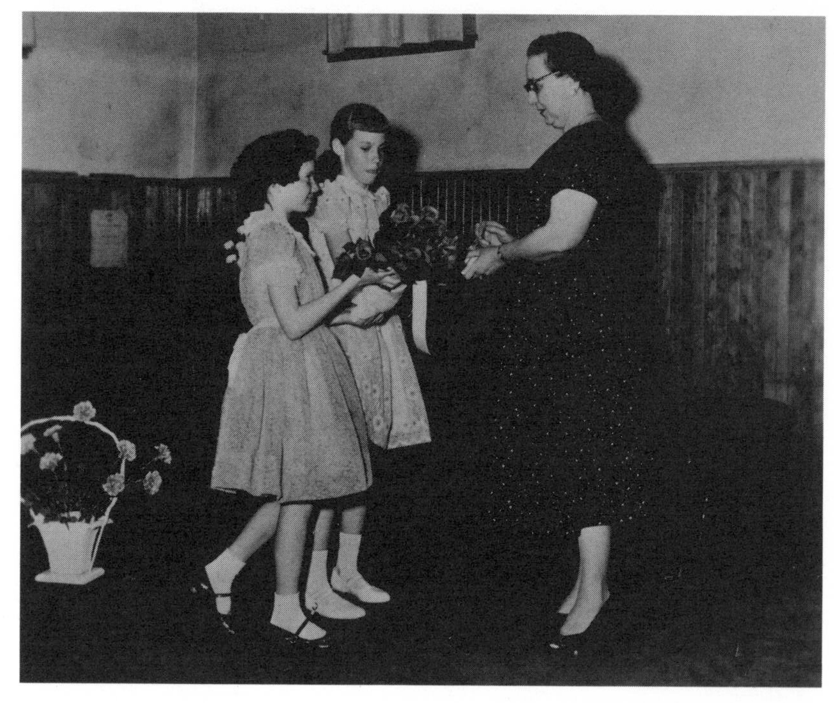

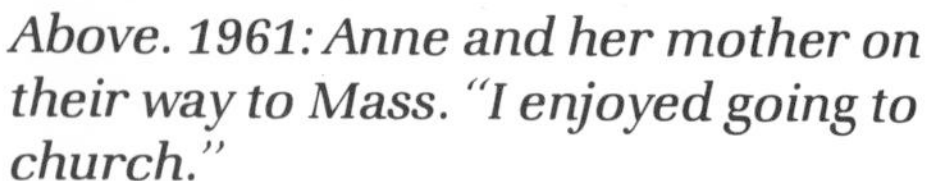

Above. 1961: Anne and her mother on their way to Mass. "I enjoyed going to church."

Above right. Anne (in the center) presents flowers to an early mentor, her piano teacher, Mrs. Jack Matthews.

Opposite. "I've always liked this picture a lot. That was taken at Maryann White's house."

all-female choral group, organized and conducted by her English teacher, Mrs. Ackie Allbon, an engagingly colorful woman who sports her opinions, like her lipstick, with enthusiasm. "No adjective is too elaborate or too endearing to do credit to Anne," she says. She recalls that Anne's voice was always distinctively deep and full and that on *Supper Club*, a local television show on which her group sometimes performed, Anne's first three solos were "Moon River," "Brahms' Lullabye," and "The Hawaiian Wedding Song." In English class, she was an "excellent student" and, highest of all praise, she was never "show-offish." In a small mining town like Springhill it might have been easy for a doctor's kids to give themselves airs, but "Dr. Murray never let any of them think they were better than anybody."

Before Anne Murray, Springhill made headlines with its hard luck: coal mining disasters in 1891, 1956, 1958; a fire on Main Street in 1957. Against such a backdrop of picturesque misfortune, it is tempting to present Anne's early life as a sentimental education in survival. But it seems a little simplistic to suggest that Anne Murray is down-to-earth because she had friends whose fathers were killed in the pit. Moreover, residents of Springhill, like many Maritimers, grow tired of being depicted as inhabitants of a land of the perpetually disadvantaged.

Anne herself has no easy explanation of what it means to

be from the Maritimes. Searching to summarize the significance of where she grew up, she offers, "I think, it's not taking yourself that seriously. It's a sense of humor and an attitude — no matter what happens, it's not that important. You're just one little thing in the whole scheme of things."

Mrs. Marion Murray, April 1981. Lots of people say that that's exactly what Anne will look like when she grows older.

Opposite. The photographer who took this early publicity picture remembers how pleasant Anne was to work with. Photographers who have worked with her since say the same.

three

It All Started with Snowbird

AT HER high school graduation in 1962, Anne Murray sang "Ava Maria." Encouraged by her mother, she enrolled at Mount St. Vincent, a Catholic women's college in Halifax, which she has described as being both a fortress and a prison. During a rehearsal for a campus revue, a nun took perplexing exception to Anne's rendition of "Summertime." "She thought I sounded black. She asked me to do it differently." Anne, who can count on one hand the number of times she's wept in the last ten years, cried her eyes out.

The summer after Mount St. Vincent, Anne got a job at the Keltic Lodge in Ingonish, Nova Scotia. During time off from maid duties, she and a couple of fellow staffers formed a group, and on a few occasions they entertained guests at the lodge, singing songs by Peter, Paul and Mary and the Kingston Trio.

In the fall, Anne started work on a degree in physical education at the University of New Brunswick in Fredericton. In the three years she was there she twice took part in the annual Red and Black Revue. "I still remember going down to

1967: An early publicity shot from Singalong Jubilee. *In the early years Anne strummed as well as sang but she hasn't played the guitar in performance since 1973. "The guitar was a crutch for me. I always felt I could get into a song better if I had the guitar."*

audition. I thought there'd be millions of people better than I was, but my roommate and friends said, 'You're crazy. Get down there.' When I got there, I realized there weren't a lot of people better than I was."

Less successfully, in the summer of 1964 Anne tried out for *Singalong Jubilee*, a CBC summer television series out of Halifax. However, they already had more altos than they could use. Instead, the Fredericton Curling Club provided gigs, and Anne sometimes sang there for twenty-five dollars a night. In her graduating year, she got a call from Bill Langstroth, *Singalong* host. She auditioned again and made her debut on the series on her twenty-first birthday, in 1966.

For years, Langstroth had produced a show featuring Don Messer, whose down-east, barn-dance music had become an emblem of Maritime culture. As a summer replacement for that weekly favorite, Langstroth produced a pilot with Pete Seeger in 1960. When the CBC decided that the activist folk singer was too hot politically, *Singalong Jubilee* was born. It combined the good-natured hijinks of a hootenanny with the good intentions of a folk mass. Langstroth hosted, in a determinedly off-the-cuff style, and introduced a variety of Maritime talents, many of whom sang and played guitar. To start, Anne was one of the chorus who sat around in casual arrangements, decked out in the latest anti-establishment fashion to have reached Halifax—granny glasses, dolly dresses and love beads. But the show had a callow innocence and, more significant, revealed to the rest of Canada that not all music in the Maritimes was made on fiddles.

After a year of teaching phys. ed. at Athena Regional High School in Prince Edward Island, Anne moved to Halifax to become a featured soloist on *Singalong*. She also appeared on a CBC teen series called *Let's Go*. Her fame grew, and other engagements followed. She played to capacity crowds at the Orient Lounge in Antigonish. The Monterey Lounge in Halifax billed her as the "star of television," and in April of 1968, when she performed in a variety concert in Halifax, the Springhill paper reported, "Dr. J.C. Murray and Mrs. Murray, accompanied by their son Bruce, motored to Halifax Sunday to attend 'Starcast '68.' "

Besides exposure, Anne gained from *Singalong* her first manager, Bill Langstroth, and her first record producer, Brian Ahern. Ahern now owns his own company in Los Angeles,

Another publicity shot from Singalong. *Despite Anne's poetic gaze, her feet, as always, were planted firmly on the ground.*

Anne and other Singalong Jubilee regulars, including Bill Langstroth in the overalls. Seated in front: the late Fred McKenna (he introduced Anne to country music), and standing behind: Catherine McKinnon, Jim Bennett and Anne. While Singalong was mostly done in the studio, some segments, usually of a comic nature, were shot outside and edited into the program.

Opposite. "YOUNG MARITIME SINGER: Vivacious young Anne Murray is the featured singer on Sounds '68 *from Halifax for four successive Saturdays on CBC television." Publicity portrait and caption from CBC.*

producing records by his wife, Emmylou Harris, and others. But back in the sixties he was *Singalong's* musical director and a go-getter. As one former colleague remembers, "Brian was always the kid sitting around reading *How to Make a Million*." Already a guitarist, jingle writer and musical director, Ahern moved to Toronto in 1967 and learned to produce records. Still going back to Halifax to work on *Singalong Jubilee* in the summers, during the rest of the year he worked in Toronto for Arc Records, one of the first Canadian record companies. Finally conceding to Ahern's repeated urging that she should come to Toronto and cut wax, Anne went in the summer of 1968. She had already appeared on a *Singalong* cast album that Arc had put out, but this was her first solo stint in the studio.

What About Me was released in the fall of 1968. It was, as Bill Langstroth's liner notes suggested, a mixture of "folk" and "contemporary" with several songs written by such Canadians as Ian Tyson, Joni Mitchell and David Wiffen. However,

"That was from the series of shows that Bill did. Bill produced and directed a series of fifteen-minute shows called Sounds '68. . . . *That's a great suit. I used to love that suit."*

Anne signs copies of her first album in a Springhill shop in September 1968. When that store ran out of its stock of three hundred, Anne moved down the street and continued signing a fresh supply at another establishment.

Opposite. While working at St. Mary's University, Leonard Rambeau, now Anne's manager, penned an article for Campus *magazine, January 1970. He wrote: "The face is a mirror, sad yet often sunny, and the magical voice can echo a thousand years of despair—and match the mischievous ebullience of a Huckleberry Finn."*

those were the days when you could still tell a Canadian album by looking at it. *What About Me* had a certain primitive quality of graphics and sound that was then the state of the art for the Canadian recording industry, and perhaps only to be expected from an album that cost three thousand dollars to make. In November, Anne made her first Springhill stage appearance since "Ava Maria," and the local press went crazy. "At first there was a gasp of delight at how sophisticated the young star looked in her glamorous, shiny hostess gown in the Mandarin style. This was immediately followed by delighted laughter as it became obvious that tomboy Anne was barefoot."

Paul White, in charge of signing up new artists to Capitol Records Canada, was also struck by the barefoot singer on *Singalong Jubilee*, and his interest coincided with Anne's

Anne and Gene MacLellan, "Snowbird" composer.

In September 1970, Anne flew from Halifax International Airport to California to tape her first appearance on Glen Campbell's television show. Left to right: Anne's mother, Anne, a flight attendant, and Anne's father.

search for a new record company, one with American connections. They had a meeting in Toronto, and a week later the contract was signed. Capitol gave her artistic licence and eighteen thousand dollars, Brian Ahern produced, and *This Way Is My Way* was released in the fall of 1969. In the course of the following year came "Snowbird," Anne's first and biggest international hit.

As a single, "Snowbird" was released in the United States in March 1970. It was a dizzying success around the globe. Although in rehearsal Anne and the band may poke fun at it now, perhaps turning its breezy melody into a supercharged polka, the song remains a signature piece. And Anne remains forever grateful for the day Bill Langstroth called her up and said he had, in the course of his duties as producer of the *Don Messer Show*, come across this songwriter called Gene MacLellan. Anne gave a listen, chose "Snowbird," and before you knew it she was, as they say in the record business, "bubbling under."

four

Making It

CELERY, olives, pickles. Baked ham and roast turkey. Potato salad. Cole slaw. Buttered rolls. Strawberry shortcake. Thus unfolded the testimonial dinner that highlighted Anne Murray's triumphant homecoming in July 1971. Prime Minister Pierre Trudeau had sent a telegram: "Your singing has made our hearts lighter and our lives happier." Anne was so besieged by autograph hounds that she fled to Prince Edward Island under cover of a black wig borrowed from her guitarist's wife. At age twenty-six, Anne Murray was a star, the likes of which neither her hometown nor her native country had ever known.

Besides inciting journalists to a thousand and one cute metaphors about spreading wings and taking flight, "Snowbird" set off one of the busiest years of Anne's life. By June 1970, it was on the charts both in Canada and the United States. In early July, the CBC director of entertainment programs announced that Anne had been signed to an exclusive two-year radio and television contract. On September 7th, when she left Halifax bound for Los Angeles and the first of several regular appearances on the *Glen Campbell Goodtime Hour*, crowds turned up at the airport to see her off. In November, she was presented with her first gold record on the *Merv Griffin Show*, and in December, she performed at Toronto's Royal York Hotel in the Imperial Room, the best-known nightclub in the country.

For the sake of convenience, Anne moved to Toronto in

July, 1971. Anne rides through the streets of Springhill, Nova Scotia.

early 1971. But the twenty-second-floor high-rise apartment on Balliol Street, with its yellow and orange leather furniture, didn't see that much of her. During the first four months of 1971, she spent two weeks at home. In February there was a gig with Glen Campbell at Harrah's in Lake Tahoe. Then there was a string of one-nighters in the prairie provinces, followed by a week at The Cave, a club in Vancouver, British Columbia. During that week, Anne flew to Los Angeles to sing on the Grammy show (she was nominated in two categories) and flew to the moon on tranquilizers. "I was a complete and total wreck. A doctor who had gone to school with my brother gave me some very light tranquilizers, and I used them that week. That was that. I've never used them since, cause they put me right out of it."

The year after "Snowbird" was not only one of the busiest of Anne's life. It was also the one that she has come to call "the worst." Her schedule left her mind in an uproar; she said yes

Anne appears with Canadian talk-show host Elwood Glover in 1972.

Anne in front of her first house, distorted by a fisheye lens. It took some time before Anne could adjust to the fact that she had made it. More than once she told reporters of sitting in the backyard wondering how she ever came to own a pool.

Taping for a CBC special in April 1973, Anne toured northern Manitoba, the Yukon and Northwest Territories with fellow Maritime performer John Allan Cameron. "The tour was kind of therapeutic for me. It came at a time when I thought that I was just a one-hit wonder."

to everything. Like her mother and her brother Bruce, Anne does not enjoy flying. In March 1971, as a headline in the Vancouver *Sun* proclaimed, she was "In the air everywhere, 24 hours a day." In another headline, the Montreal *Gazette* bluntly stated, "Anne Murray has to learn how to relax."

By the middle of 1971, Anne no longer had the time to make her own travel arrangements and issue her own checks. She turned her books, or, more precisely, her brown paper bags full of receipts, over to Lyman MacInnis, a prominent

Kenny Loggins, Anne and Jim Messina. Anne's fretting about being a one-hit wonder was allayed by "Danny's Song" (penned by Loggins) which won her a 1973 Grammy nomination for Best Pop Female Vocal Performance. In 1975 "Love Song" (penned by Loggins and Messina) won her a Grammy for Best Country Female Vocal Performance.

Glen Campbell guested with Anne on one of her television specials aired in November 1972. In 1973 she toured the United Kingdom and Germany with him.

chartered accountant from Prince Edward Island whose other clients included hockey stars Bobby Hull and Norm Ullman. Anne also formed a company, Balmur Limited, to establish the order so far missing from her business affairs, and eventually to handle other artists. The "Mur" was a nickname from college; "B" was for Brian Ahern and Bill Langstroth, her record and television producers; "A" was for Anne, the president; and "L" was for Leonard T. Rambeau. In 1968 and 1969, Rambeau, from Smelt Brook, Nova Scotia, had arranged concerts in Dartmouth and Halifax. Impressed by his efficiency, Anne had promised him that if she ever had need of a road manager, she would call him. In May 1971 Rambeau left his government job with Canada Manpower and moved to Toronto. Key to his managerial style is an insistence on doing things right, and doing them big. In May 1976 he was made president of Balmur.

Nowadays, Balmur is what Anne means when she says "the office." It is the main conduit of her business and serves as a guardhouse against trespassers into her life as a private citizen. However, to pretend that her career was always so stable would be to contradict the facts. Indeed, Anne was making enough money to buy lavish Christmas presents in 1971 (a dishwasher for her mother; a TV with remote control for her father). In 1972 she purchased a house in a swank part of Toronto for $90,000. The price now seems to be an old-fashioned idea of expensive, but back then it was big enough to signify success. However, although materially rewarding, her career lacked momentum. It was more than two years after "Snowbird" before Anne put out a single that could be described as a follow-up hit.

Recognition for Anne came in diverse forms. In early 1973 she visited the Canadian Forces base in Chatham, New Brunswick, where, celebrating their twenty-fifth anniversary, the Lynx squadron declared her an honorary lynx.

By the time "Danny's Song" was headed for the top ten in the spring of 1973, Anne was in the position of being overexposed in Canada and underexposed in the United States. Thanks to new government regulations that made it mandatory for Canadian radio stations to air a certain percentage of Canadian music, "Snowbird" had been played so much that even Gene MacLellan, the man who wrote it, told a reporter that he was "pretty sick of it." Thanks to the CBC's eagerness to prove that it could create a star, Anne's face was as familiar as the test pattern on Canadian television. In the spring of 1973 Anne decided not to renew her CBC contract and turned her attention to the American market.

Left to right: John Lennon, Anne, Harry Nilsson, Alice Cooper and ex-Monkee Mickey Dolenz at the Troubadour in November 1973, one of the most highly publicized gigs of Anne's career. Even New York's Women's Wear Daily, *chronicle of fashion and society, reported: "Lennon in a mellow mood said the music was 'just lovely' and the food 'great.'"*

Opposite. In London in 1973, Anne taped a special for BBC television.

While Anne was grateful for the advantages that came from being associated with Glen Campbell—in addition to doing his television show, she toured Europe with him and played Vegas where a furrier gave her a discount on a sporty white mink when he found out she was with the Campbell show—she also worried about possible adverse effects. Identification with Campbell reinforced an unwanted "country" label. She wasn't sure that Nick Sevano, Campbell's manager, was the right manager for her as well. Talking about Sevano in a magazine interview in July 1973, Anne said, "It got to the point where I had to call him and say, 'Nick, it's not a fruitful relationship. Nothing's happening...I have no gigs in the U.S.'"

Anne hired Shep Gordon, well-known in the industry for his packaging of rock star Alice Cooper, and played one of the most highly publicized gigs of her career. Gordon, with great pageantry, booked her into the Troubadour in Los Angeles for the American Thanksgiving, November 1973. Parchment invitations were delivered by hand. The audience was studded with celebs and there were gallons of wine. Anne had her picture taken with John Lennon and emerged on stage out of a large wooden turkey. In short, it was a remarkably long way from celery, olives and pickles in Springhill, Nova Scotia.

Like her voice with its instantly recognizable sadness, Anne's face in performance sometimes registers an aching melancholy.

Opposite. In 1974 Anne was a guest on a television special, Back to the Ranch, *starring the rock group Chicago.*

five

No Trespassing

IN 1974, the general perception of Anne Murray was that she had gone funky. She said, "You bet your ass," and sounded gutsy on her latest album, *Love Song*. She appeared on *Midnight Special*, a weekly rock show; performed in New York's Central Park with Bruce Springsteen as an opening act; and curled her hair. While Shep Gordon made media fodder of her career, the press carried on endlessly with glib, cynical accounts of a new image, as if it hadn't been clear from the titles of her very first albums, *What About Me* and *This Way Is My Way*, that Anne's nature had a decidedly cocky aspect.

However, the real demonstration of Anne's spunk had nothing to do with her career. It was revealed in her wedding. On June 20, 1975, her thirtieth birthday, she married Bill Langstroth. The service was performed at home by a priest. The papers didn't know anything about it for days. It was even a surprise for Anne's parents. They had come to Toronto planning only to attend a Canada Music Day luncheon honoring their daughter. Caught unprepared, the mother of the bride had to wear the one dressy outfit she had brought with her, the same one she had worn two days earlier to lunch. The bride herself wore green and went shoeless.

In asserting her tastes for privacy and informality, it was as if Anne was declaring herself independent of all the forces that had ever tried to make of her something she wasn't. While professionally she may have had to endure the machinations

In 1974 the Canadian music industry awarded Anne another Juno as Female Vocalist of the Year. It was her fourth consecutive win in that category. Standing behind Anne are the presenters, Kathy Young and Burton Cummings.

Opposite. In March 1975 Anne received a Grammy for "Love Song."

of a hype-hungry manager, she remained in charge of her private life. Before news of the wedding broke, fans might have guessed that she would marry Leonard Rambeau. An attentive manager and close friend, he was frequently seen by her side. But, although her affair with Bill Langstroth, a married man fifteen years her senior, had stirred village gossip in Halifax where their relationship started, Anne managed to keep the romance a private matter. Some members of the press knew of it but, following Anne's discreet lead, kept quiet.

Bill Langstroth still prefers to keep a low profile. Interview Anne in the kitchen and Bill removes himself to the living room, not in the obsequious way of a Mr. Murray, but gladly, like somebody with other and better things to do. He sometimes helps write Anne's stage material, but over the years has detached himself from her business, and from show business in general. Asked about his background in broadcasting, he dismisses it as a story that would take too long to tell. More inclined to talk about current prospects, he speaks of a variety of interests: photography, Dale Carnegie, plans for a company that would market family portraits, done on video rather than traditional still cameras. The father of a grown son and daughter from his previous marriage, he is a seasoned but still

Anne co-produced the first album by her brother Bruce who in August of 1975 sang a duet with her at the grandstand of the Canadian National Exhibition in Toronto. To the charges of nepotism that some critics made, Anne says simply, "We're family. We've always been close even as little kids."

Anne with Bill Langstroth on Singalong Jubilee.

Opposite. Anne and John Denver backstage at the Canadian National Exhibition in 1975.

June 20, 1975. The bride and the mother-of-the-bride. Before Dr. and Mrs. Murray left Springhill to attend a luncheon in Toronto, Anne had told her parents on the phone that she had a surprise in store. The surprise later made headlines: "Anne Murray Secretly Wed."

Opposite. Anne's wedding was the height of informality. She can't remember where she got the dress, only that she originally bought it for lounging and ended up getting married in it. The cake was chocolate, by Sara Lee.

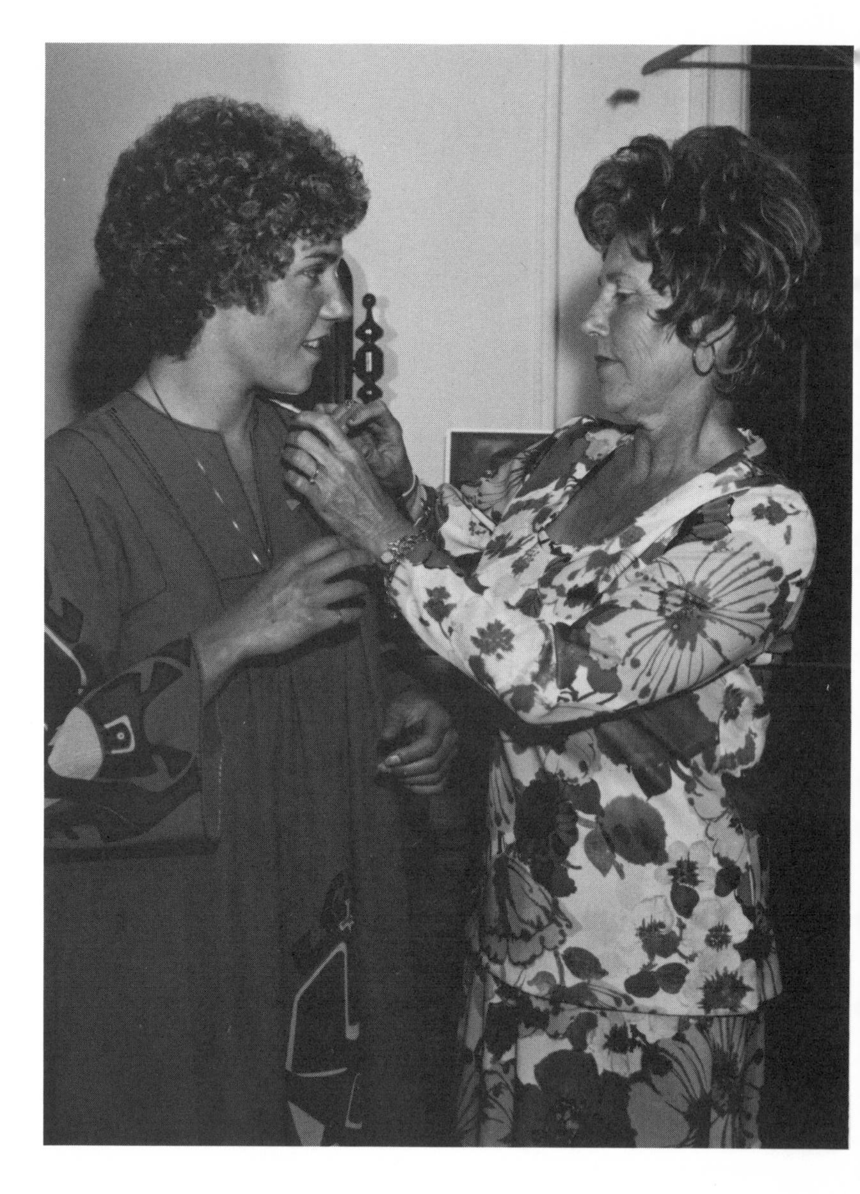

bright-eyed parent. He is most exuberant talking about the importance of making sure that children are encouraged to be creative.

William Langstroth was born in August 1976; his sister Dawn arrived in April 1979. Lest their lives be somehow polluted by her fame, Anne tries to keep their upbringing "as normal as possible." The first time William saw his mother perform was on his fourth birthday. But when Anne led three thousand people in rousing chorus of "Happy Birthday" from the stage of Toronto's O'Keefe Centre, she allowed no lights to be turned on her son in the audience. On the rare occasions when she and Bill have permitted magazines to publish photographs of the children, they have insisted on side-and/or rear-angle shots.

It could be argued that such cautious measures, while necessary and admirably protective, are inadvertently teasing and create mystery where ordinarily there wouldn't be any. Because it's forbidden, the very idea of a frontal shot of one of Anne Murray's kids is almost pornographic. Even Anne herself wonders why the press is wont to make such a fuss over her children. "You never hear anything about Dinah Shore's children or Perry Como's children." The obvious answer is that, to an unusual degree, Anne has repeatedly declared motherhood a higher priority than her profession. In April

Besides several gold and platinum records, Anne has also received more solemn recognition. In 1975 the Canadian government named her an Officer of the Order of Canada. Anne poses with Margaret and Pierre Trudeau following the ceremony.

Opposite. September 1976: Mother and baby doing fine.

Above. Anne arrives at the Tokyo airport in 1977.

Above right. Canada's number one singer with Japan's number one sumo wrestler in Tokyo, 1977.

1979 she was quoted in *US Magazine*: "As soon as I built my career around my family life, everything—the career and my own feelings about myself—improved."

In November 1975, when Anne learned that she was pregnant for the first time, it was announced that she was coming off the road. Anne now speaks of a period of "semi-retirement" that lasted until she re-emerged in full sail in 1978. But although it was a time of lying low, it was not altogether inactive. A promoter sued her for allegedly having reneged on a contract to appear at a state fair. Settlement was reached out of court. There were records, television specials and some concerts. In 1977 Anne sang and, with her musical director Pat

Boy scouts attending a jamboree in Prince Edward Island were featured on a CBC Superspecial broadcast in October 1977.

Riccio Jr., helped produce *There's a hippo in my tub*, an album of children's songs released in the United States by Sesame Street Records. In the same year she also toured Japan where she was called "Canada's Sweetheart," "Canada's Olivia Newton-John," and where, less damagingly, one writer said that she blew away the gloom of the rainy season. And late in 1977 Anne undertook a gig even more notorious than jumping out of the turkey at the Troubadour when, joining the ranks of Carmelita Pope and Ricardo Montalban, she became a commercial spokesperson.

For some people, when Anne Murray signed a contract to do print and television advertisements for the Canadian Imperial Bank of Commerce, that was the end of Anne Murray; she had sold out. Although Anne had never assumed the airs of social relevance the way some of her contemporaries did, she did start off singing songs by Bob Dylan, Eric Anderson and Tom Paxton. And while it requires a rather doctrinaire attitude to regard doing bank ads as a political gesture, there is some bemusing irony to think that in 1968, on her first album, Anne was singing about trails of trouble and

In 1977 the president of the University of New Brunswick presented Anne with an Honorary Doctor of Letters degree from her alma mater.

At a press conference prior to her sold-out concerts in Halifax in July 1977.

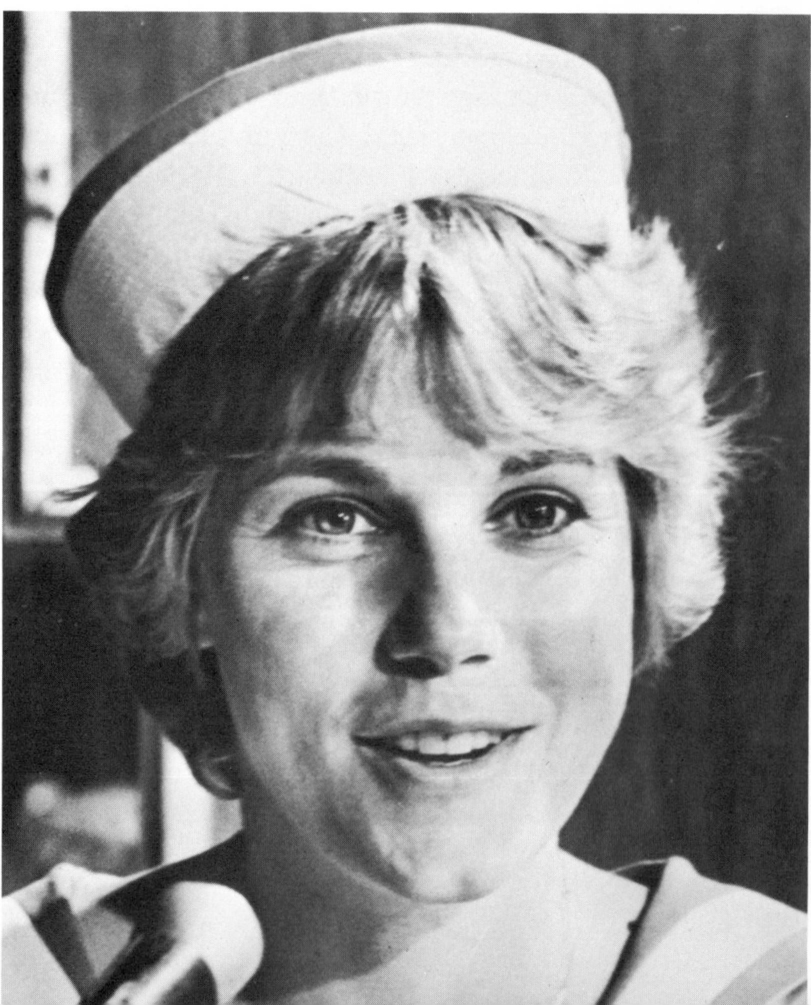

In March 1978 Anne was a participant in NBC's First Annual Rock and Roll Sports Classic.

"Paths of Victory." At a 1977 press conference in Halifax when she discussed her involvement with the bank, Anne said that the money would enable her to spend more time as a mother and less time on the road.

six

This Way Is My Way

WHILE it may be appropriately dramatic to describe Anne Murray's re-entry into the limelight in 1978 as a comeback, it is not entirely accurate. She had never really been away and, more to the point, with "You Needed Me," a number one hit which appeared on a 1978 album entitled *Let's Keep It That Way*, Anne achieved such new heights of renown that everything before it seemed preliminary. More copies of both the single and the album were sold than of anything she had ever released. "You Needed Me" won Anne a Grammy in the pop category and, once and for all, freed her from the confines of the "country singer" label.

In late 1975 Anne had made a deliberate effort to go pop. After making ten albums with Brian Ahern, she went to California to work with producer Tom Catalano, who had produced such city types as Peggy Lee and Neil Diamond. With Catalano on the boards, Anne recorded *Together* and *Keeping in Touch*. The L.A. recording sessions were heavy-handed affairs, with the record company wielding its authority. Capitol Records not only pushed for Catalano, but also pressured Anne to record material she didn't like. Anne found

Anne cooks with Diane Brooks and Laurel Ward. Brooks, a regular back-up singer with Anne in the early years, summarizes Anne in brief words — "a beautiful lady."

herself at odds with Catalano's way of doing things. "Tom would choose the songs, and he would say, 'Well, I think we ought to get Artie Butler [an arranger] for these three songs, and for these we should have Michael Omartian [another arranger]. And he would send these songs out, and they would get arranged. By the time I got to the studio, they were there. That was it. Even the parts for the steel guitars were written, and that for me was too structured. I felt I could have phoned in my part of it." In fact, *Keeping in Touch* even looks so perfunctory that you're not surprised to learn that it's the least favorite of Anne's albums. On the back of the album are no credits, only a postcard, mailed in Springhill and addressed to Capitol Records in Hollywood, on which Anne suggests how the cuts on the album should be ordered: "Here's the tune stack as I see it:. . . O.K.?"

Anne's current background vocalists are Debbie Schall Greimann and Bruce Murray, Las Vegas 1980. Anne herself has done back-up duty on albums by Bruce, Dianne Brooks, Mary Kay Place and Jesse Winchester. "I'm a big fan of back-up vocals. I like to push them way up so that you can really hear them, but sometimes you can't talk producers into that."

In the studio in the fall of 1977 Anne goes over material with producer Jim Ed Norman. Prior to working with Anne, Norman had produced "Right Time of the Night" for Jennifer Warnes who sang on the soundtrack of Norma Rae *which starred Sally Field. Burt Reynolds once arranged for Anne to sing the song "You Needed Me" to Field over the phone.*

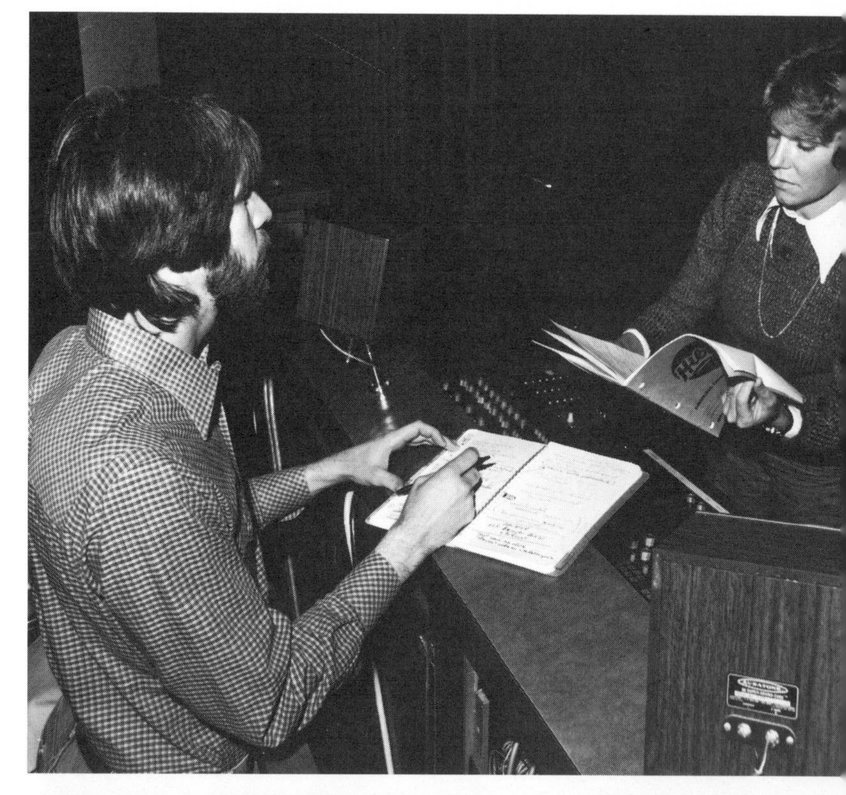

Left to right: Jim Ed Norman, Anne and Randy Goodrum, composer of "You Needed Me," the song with which Anne won her Grammy for Best Pop Female Vocal Performance. In 1978, "You Needed Me" was named Song of the Year both by the Nashville Songwriters Association and by the Academy of Country Music. Goodrum also wrote "Broken Hearted Me."

Opposite. In the summer of 1978 Anne became the first solo musical performer to play Toronto's venerable Royal Alexandra Theatre. "An Evening with Anne Murray" sold out for a week.

Reverting to old habits, Anne bares her foot on the star unveiled in 1975 at Nashville's Country Music Hall of Fame Walkway of Stars.

In the summer of 1980, a star in Anne's honor was unveiled in Hollywood. At the mike to express her gratitude, Anne began with her usual self-mockery: "I'm really good at this. This'll be a killer."

Backstage after Anne performed at The Roxy in Los Angeles, 1978. Left to right: Bernadette Peters, Kim Carnes, Anne and Dusty Springfield.

The warmest memory Anne has of working with Tom Catalano is working with Dusty Springfield and Dianne Brooks. They did back-up vocals on *Together*. "For a whole week, I was in heaven," Anne recalls, "singing with these two women." She had always held Springfield in the highest esteem and speaks of her voice as "one of the finest instruments in the world." And Anne's admiration for Dianne Brooks as a singer and a friend was not news to anybody who had read the liner notes on *Danny's Song*: "This album is dedicated to Dianne Gwendolyn Brooks who has been a constant source of inspiration." On record, perhaps Brooks' most noticeable contribution was made on *Annie*. It is her voice—sweet, dark and stretchy like taffy—that you hear breathing fire in the background of "Robbie's Song for Jesus."

Anne's sold-out engagement at Carnegie Hall in 1979 was another signal of new heights attained.

Anne and Rodney Dangerfield, with whom she has shared the bill at the Riviera in Las Vegas, were presenters and winners at the 1980 Grammy Awards ceremony. Dangerfield won in the comedy category.

It was also she who taught Anne the ropes of backphrasing, a bluesy technique that Anne put to splendid use on "Backstreet Lovin'," possibly the closest she's ever come to raunch.

Released in 1974 on *Love Song*, "Backstreet Lovin'" endures as a tribute to how good Anne can be when she chooses to sound tough, and to how well she and Brian Ahern could work together. But, although it placed on the country charts, its success was less than meteoric. Lots of people, including Dianne Brooks, prefer Anne's mellow tones, epitomized in "You Needed Me" and other such ballads that became her trademark after 1978. "You Needed Me," like more

than half the songs which wound up on Anne's *Greatest Hits* album, was produced by Jim Ed Norman, whom Anne describes as a happy medium between Tom Catalano, overwhelmingly efficient, and Brian Ahern, sympathetic and chaotic. "I think Brian and I were a lot more adventurous than I am now. As a matter of fact, I know we were. Some of the things we did were really off the wall. And I loved it, but they didn't sell anything. It wasn't until I really did the straight ahead kind of thing that people started buying."

Undoubtedly, the years since 1978 have been the most prosperous of Anne's career. Besides a regular income from her endorsements for the Bank of Commerce (a sum that both she and the bank are bound by contract not to disclose), and the more than eight million albums she sold between 1979 and 1981, there was also a multi-million-dollar deal with the Riviera Hotel in Las Vegas. And although she admits to being broke in 1976 (the accumulated effect of ill-advised bookings, lack of record company support in the United States and keeping musicians on retainer) even then she didn't have to liquidate assets. Following the advice of her accountant, Lyman MacInnis, Anne has secure investments in blue-chip stock. She also owns property. Although she has sold the motel in Prince Edward Island where she and Bill honeymooned in 1975, she has a house in Toronto and owns fifteen acres of undeveloped coastline near Peggy's Cove, Nova Scotia.

Not one to gauge her welfare solely by economic factors, Anne also prizes peace of mind, which for her comes with a feeling of being in control. After years of fitful management, she sat down with Leonard Rambeau and agent Fred Lawrence in late 1977 to plan a career course. Balmur Limited reduced its roster of other artists it represented and concentrated on Anne. Leonard Rambeau rented an apartment in Los Angeles because he was spending so much time there. In the fall of 1979, also for the purposes of making inroads into the American market, Anne undertook a promotional blitz. She appeared on *Dinah*, *Mike Douglas*, *Phil Donahue* and the *Today Show*. She consented to an article in *People* magazine that included pictures of her home and children. In October 1979 there was a twenty-four page advertising supplement in *Billboard*, the music industry's trade journal. Abandoning the struggle of trying to pretend that the music business was something other than strategy, Anne sensibly decided to rec-

Opposite. Anne displays her 1980 Grammy for "Could I Have This Dance?" winner of the Best Country Female Vocal Performance category.

ognize Caesar's things. At the same time, she gained renewed pleasure from singing. While concerts in such auspicious venues as Carnegie Hall, Radio City Music Hall, the Palladium in London, and the Royal Alexandra Theatre in Toronto may have been planned by Leonard Rambeau because they were high profile, that was not the reason they sold out. People went to see Anne enjoy herself in a way she had never been able to before—a way that was most definitely her own.

Toronto, November 1979. As honorary chairperson (1979-1980) for the Canadian Save the Children Fund, Anne attended a dinner in aid of that charitable organization along with Princess Anne, honorary chairperson from Britain.

Opposite. "I always feel that when you leave a performance, you should feel that you know the performer a little better."

seven

Fame, Fortune and Fashion

THERE are some people to whom any talk of image is quite simply rude. However, to discuss Anne Murray and not talk about her image is impossible. From the very beginning, she has endured such fixed preconceptions about who she is and what she stands for that some journalist is always rushing into print to announce a "new" Anne Murray.

To start, Anne was pegged as the girl-next-door who just happened to have a voice like nobody else's. She was the schoolmarm turned folksinger, all blonde and fresh-faced and virtuous. On the first album she made for Capitol, the liner notes presented her as a reminder that "this is still a nice world to live in," and for years the press made her seem too good to be true. As early as 1970, at a press conference in Toronto, Anne cracked to one reporter, "Hey, why don't you write something rotten about me?" Again in 1973, trying to unburden herself of the role of goodness incarnate, she told an audience at the National Arts Centre in Ottawa, "I want you people to know that under these clothes and behind this facade, this body is a mass of hickeys." And in the spring of 1981, she released an album, *Where Do You Go When You Dream*, that was another send-up of her saintly image. On the

"Grade nine. I can tell from the pin curls. Hair just out of the pin curls. Really cute."

"They had me in all different costumes and different hairstyles," Anne says, remembering Sounds '68. *"I was a little chunkier then."*

Accompanied by Bill Langstroth, Anne performs at a reception in Saint John, New Brunswick. In a mini, verging on micro, Anne was not the only one to reflect those gamier days.

front she posed with cherubs, and in the photograph on the back, wearing lacquered nails and painted mouth, she looked like the confirmation of every mother's worst fears for her daughter.

From time to time there have been writers who have tried to suggest a steamier side of Anne Murray. Reviewing the album, *Danny's Song*, American rock critic Lester Bangs called Anne "a hypnotically compelling interpretrix with a voice like molten highschool rings and a heavy erotic vibe." However, for the most part, people still remember Anne as the girl who used to go barefoot. In fact, in the old days, when Anne performed without shoes, more attention could not have been paid to her feet had she strummed guitar with them. One reporter, reviewing an early concert, felt obliged to point out that "Anne now beats time with her big toe, instead of her

Short, shag, curled...
there are those who can
trace Anne's career
by her coiffure.

Anne cites this marabou jacket by Juul Haalmeyer as the kind of thing that makes her feel like a million dollars. She wore the jacket for the first time when she guested on The Muppet Show *in January 1980.*

Anne originally bought this T-shirt in Los Angeles as a gift for Bill. It shrank when it was washed and she ended up with it.

Segments of Anne's first television special in 1970 were shot in Peggy's Cove, Nova Scotia.

Anne in her first apartment in Toronto, 1971.

Anne describes her favorite state as "that feeling of selflessness when you realize just how insignificant you are and who cares anyway?"

"I feel most real in Nova Scotia. That's where I feel like me to me."

Opposite. Hamilton Place, Hamilton, Ontario, January 1981.

In the early years Anne was still wearing the coat she had in grade ten.

Opposite. Anne doesn't like having her picture taken any more than her mother does, but photo sessions are a regular and unavoidable part of show business. "I've become numb to having my picture taken. I realize that it's part of the business, but that doesn't mean I have to like it."

whole foot as before." A 1970 feature article in *The War Cry*, albeit a publication of the Salvation Army, was even moved to cite scripture: "How beautiful upon the mountains are the feet of him that bringeth good tidings."

If Anne's barefoot habit signified anything other than a wish to be comfortable, it was an attitude more irreverent than holy, that same independent spirit which she expressed in 1971 when she vowed that she would never again play the International Hotel in Las Vegas. "They want you to wear shoes and they don't want you to wear hot pants because it'll hurt their image and, you know, the whole bit. . . . That's not for me." Since then, Anne has thrown her hot pants into the garbage—"just where they should have been then," she jokes—and has come to appreciate that dressing for the stage is a serious matter: "It's embarrassing to me now that I didn't know enough, but I just had no awareness about clothes. I never paid any attention to that kind of thing. I never thought it was important. I always thought that your personality and your talent were the most important things."

"Zap! And it's a new Anne Murray," proclaimed a headline in the Toronto Star, *April 1974, making it all sound easy. "Everyone's always looking for a hook for me," says Anne, "because of my image, so straight and clean and all the rest of it."*

Opposite. Performing with the Toronto Symphony at Massey Hall in 1973, Anne wears an elaborate creation that has since been sent to the Country Music Wax Museum in Nashville.

"My mother tried, God bless her, she tried. From the time I was two, she put dresses on me and I'd come home with them all ripped and covered in mud." It took Patrick Reeves Aaron, however, to make Anne feel "like a million bucks."

Anne no longer dresses herself for the stage. Since 1974, when she paid $50,000 for a new wardrobe, she has put herself in professional hands. For the three years starting in 1974, a woman named Patrick Reeves Aaron designed Anne's wardrobe, and Anne says of her, "She was the first person who put me in clothes that made me feel absolutely wonderful when I came out on stage." Laboring painstaking and costly hours, Reeves designed garments with hippie-like touches that in fact were a natural evolution from barefeet: a pair of coveralls with Raggedy Andy appliquéd on the bib; a two-piece chamois ensemble decorated with floral motifs; lots of back-to-the-earth-looking ruffled sleeves.

When Anne sported her new duds, there was talk in the papers about a makeover. However, while the outward signs may have changed, Anne had not. Remembering what it was like to work with Anne, Reeves says, "It was like designing for a

At a reception after her opening at the Royal Alexandra in 1978, Anne has her picture taken with Trudy Haalmeyer (she works with her son Juul), Pat Riccio Jr., her musical director, and Juul Haalmeyer, her costume designer.

football player, but in the nicest way possible. Annie is one of the few people who really didn't care. She cared, because she knew it was important, but for herself personally, she was much happier in sweat sox and a sweat suit."

In 1978 Juul Haalmeyer became Anne's dressmaker. A costumer in the show-biz tradition of Bob Mackie, Haalmeyer introduced Anne to the mainstream glitter that Vegas audiences demand from their headliners. But he too confirms that Anne's biggest concern is ease of wear. "Anne is not a clothes horse like Ann Margaret or Cher, so once she's comfortable in something we try not to vary too much from that particular style." Haalmeyer does about fifteen pieces a year for Anne, with prices ranging from two to eight thousand dollars. Typically, he designs tailored jackets that show off Anne's terrific shoulders, and multi-gored gowns, sometimes in see-through fabrics, that show off her legs. To save her the bother of many

On a 1972 television special, Anne primps for comic R. G. Brown, one of the few of her friends who is in the business.

Opposite. "Juul has taken it one step further. He's made me almost glamorous."

fittings, he works on a custom-made, size-ten mannequin. As far as Haalmeyer is concerned, Anne is the ideal client. She's always extremely pleasant, knows what she wants, and speaks her mind. Besides making clothes for her, he also accompanies Anne when she goes shopping. In general, Haalmeyer describes Anne's taste as classic. "She would never wear anything outrageous....She is the mother of two children first, an entertainer second."

Since 1971 when she had two coats to her name—a white parka and a brown fake fur she'd been wearing since grade ten—Anne Murray has spruced herself up considerably. Her priorities, however, have not changed drastically. Except for stage and other public engagements, she still could not care less about how she looks. Stage makeup always makes her feel "like a tart," and in private she hardly wears any. As for her hair, she describes it as "sort of a dirty dishwater blonde" which she has streaked with highlights. Cheeringly indifferent to the demands of fashion, she doesn't set much store by appearance. How she feels is what's important.

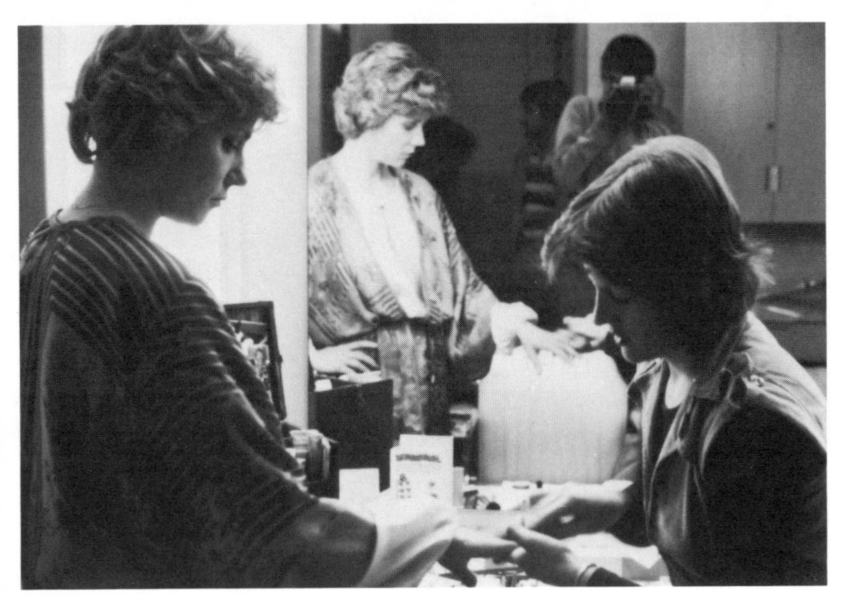

Anne submits to the demands of the television cameras.

eight

Family Life

ANNE MURRAY is not the only Canadian to have won acclaim in the United States. There have been several others, from Elizabeth Arden to Joni Mitchell. But Anne is one of the very few who have not moved away. She still makes her home in Toronto.

Far away from downtown lights, she resides in Thornhill. Located north of the city limits, Thornhill feels like a village and looks like a suburb, except the lots are bigger and the trees and hedges are more mature. The lack of sidewalks on Anne's street gives it a rural air, but otherwise it appears solid and professional. A doctor lives next door. Across the way are a husband and wife who both teach. Since moving there in early 1979, Bill has gotten to know all the neighbors. Anne is only now making their acquaintance and in fact has just started to play golf with an architect's wife from down the road.

Because Anne has drawn such a strict boundary between her professional and personal existences, it's difficult to approach her house without a sense of rare privilege. But on a warm May evening, as one walks down the drive past a neighborhood youth trimming the lawn and a Volvo with a baby's seat and stacks of newspapers bound for recycling, it seems that life at the residence of Mr. and Mrs. William Langstroth proceeds according to universal patterns.

Bill answers the door and invites me to join him in the kitchen for coffee and liqueur. Anne is off getting the kids ready for bed. William is the first out of the bath and makes an

Aged eleven, Anne practises on the piano in the parlor. The plastic on the furniture came off when people came over, but "We weren't allowed in the living room except for special occasions."

entrance in Superman pyjamas. As we are introduced, he sheepishly follows his father's instructions to shake hands. Anne appears with Dawn nestled in the crook of her arm. Dawn is blonde, with apple cheeks that could come from her mother or might be a side effect of the chicken pox she is just getting over. In any case, she's all beautiful smiles. Bill takes William off to bed and a story, and Anne goes off with Dawn, to brush her teeth and say goodnight.

Order established, Anne reappears and pulls up a stool to the table/utility area that forms an island in the middle of the kitchen. Dressed informally in a green velour track suit, she makes you feel as if she has all the time in the world, and then describes a day so full that only a tape recorder could get it all down.

Anne talks to Gordon Lightfoot after the 1974 Juno Awards. Like Anne, Lightfoot has been able to establish an international career without giving up his Toronto residence.

J.A.C.
&
MABOU RIDGE

Anne Murray: Today, I got up at eight or so, and—
David Livingstone: Does the nanny live in?
AM: Yeah...and a morning like this morning, I handed them over.
DL: And what did you do?
AM: I got up and did my exercises—
DL: Which consist of what?
AM: They consist of twenty to twenty-five minutes of exercises, head to toe. And then I do fifteen minutes on the bike, the stationary bike, and then I went golfing, played fourteen to fifteen holes of golf. Came back, and at one had a meeting with Pam at the office (Balmur's offices in Toronto).
DL: What does she take care of specifically?
AM: Well, she takes care of a lot of travel arrangements, does a lot of the itineraries, takes care of contracts. All that kind of stuff. I signed contracts and did business with Pam for a half an hour. At one thirty I had an interview (by telephone) with a radio station in St. Louis. At two I had a meeting with Bill's brother, Dave.
DL: About?
AM: We're having an addition put on the house. At four I started getting dinner ready.
DL: Which was?
AM: William had beans and weiners. Dawn had chicken and corn and yogurt. Bill had his Scarsdale, fish and yellow beans and a salad. And I had pizza. And a salad. That's four different meals. (*She laughs*.) My mother used to get us all different meals, and I always said, "Boy, that's one thing I'm never going to do." And I find myself doing it. But, with Bill eating the Scarsdale, it doesn't interest me—
DL: Then, did you—
AM: (*With mock censure*.) I'm finishing my day. Then after dinner I cleaned up the dishes and the table. Washed all the dishes and cleaned up the kitchen and took the kids up, bathed them, brushed their teeth, put them to bed. And then I came down to talk to you.

On other days, Anne forms a team with her cleaning lady Mrs. Smith and, making up for time spent away, organizes and throws things out. Even Anne's mother, who kept the living room furniture covered with plastic when her children were

Opposite. In the kitchen of her first house, Anne prepares a feed of lobsters. Some years later, when, as a guest of Mike Douglas, she gave her recipe for cooking lobsters, animal-loving viewers wrote to inform her of alternatives to the traditional method of dropping them live into boiling water.

Anne and Bill at the Heather Dunes Motel in 1973. Anne used to own the Prince Edward Island spot where she and Bill honeymooned, but gave it up because she didn't have time to oversee its upkeep.

Right. Anne and Bill party after her Carnegie Hall concert. She's now no fonder of eating in restaurants than she was as a kid. Her idea of a good time is the company of friends at home.

growing up, will tell you that Anne likes things to be shipshape. When she moved to her present address, Anne decided that she was going to take a more active part in the running of domestic affairs. Earlier, avoiding all crowd scenes, she had stopped going out to the bank or drugstore, but now she has resolved to go out shopping for whatever is needed in the way of new furniture. She also supervised the reconstruction of the kitchen. Anne's got the kind of dream kitchen that could easily be the jackpot in a contest. There are cupboards galore, with natural wood doors inset with white formica circles. You push the circle and the door springs open. The top of the table in the center of the room is also natural wood and has built into it a white formica box, containing two electrical outlets, that pops up at the touch of your hand. There are drawers deep enough to hold large pop bottles, another for holding beer; and all of them fit into a unit that can be wheeled outdoors to become a poolside refreshment stand. There are a warming oven, a standard oven, and a microwave oven, oodles of counter space, and open shelves, one of which is occupied by a collection of books: *Mary Ellen's Best of Helpful Hints, Joy of Cooking, Everyday Microwave*

Anne on holiday in the summer of 1974. An avid hockey fan, she swims, plays tennis and golf. Although feeling a little shy about whatever protocol might be involved with being a member of a club, Anne joined a golf club in the summer of 1981.

Cooking for Everyday Cooks, The Vegetarian Epicure, a cookbook compiled by the Junior League of Nashville, and one called *Out of Old Nova Scotia Kitchens* that has illustrations by a cousin of Anne's, "another one of the Mornas" in the family.

DL: Where in the house do you spend most of your time?

AM: The kitchen, and (*pointing through an opening in the wall*) this room—the TV room and living room. Upstairs we have four bedrooms. Then on this floor we have the kitchen, the living room, the dining room, Bill's office. On the next level we have another bedroom—Anne's (the nanny)—and the music room. On the next level we have a playroom. Well, why don't I show you...

DL: (*Picking up the tape recorder*.) Well, I'll take this. This'll be just like Jackie's tour of the White House.

AM: (*With mock formality*.) First, you have to come into the dining room.

At her family's cottage in Nova Scotia, Anne shells clams.

William Jr., summer 1977. After he was born in 1976, one of Anne's first gigs was a concert at the Shakespearean Festival in Stratford, Ontario.

"I think it's a magnificient kitchen," Anne says with joking pride. In December 1980, workmen were just completing it when Anne allowed a photographer from Parent's Magazine *to shoot inside her home. It was the first time a photographer had been allowed inside the house.*

The main feature of the dining room is a thick teak table with chrome supports. Like the kitchen, it was designed and executed by Bill's brother, the one who's going to be adding the extension to the house. There are large plants, leather chairs, an eighteenth-century chest of drawers and an antique Oriental rug, both inherited from Bill's grandparents who used to run an inn in Hampton, New Brunswick. On the wall is a rack of silver spoons presented to Anne when she toured the Yukon, and a set of ten prints depicting scenes from the Canadian provinces. "Scott Paper put them out for $2.98 or something."

As we pass Bill, who is sitting reading, Anne cracks, "This is an old relic I found." In the living room there are more Langstroth heirlooms which Anne describes casually. "This is an old table." "This is an old chair." There are new sofas, some old sofas that have been re-covered, on one of which is thrown an afghan crocheted by Anne's mother. There's a painting done by a Nova Scotia painter, Kelsey Raymond, who was Bill's roommate at Mount Allison University in New Brunswick, and a large school photograph of William Jr.

Anne on holiday in Northport, Nova Scotia, summer, 1977.

There are videotape equipment and a television in the living room, and another television and an impressive sound system in the music room. There are shelves of records with a special section reserved for some of Anne's favorites and labeled "The Beatles Dusty Nilsson." Anne is the only one who ever bothers to put them back in the right place. In the playroom there are a set of child-sized drums, a record player, a little rocking chair, a little toy piano that was a gift from Debbie Schall Greimann (she sings back-up with Anne), and big blocks of foam, designed by Bill and his handy brother.

The last stop on the tour is the bomb shelter which Anne has had turned into a storage area with lots of open shelves filled with antique bric-a-brac and stacks of awards. "You've seen one, and you've seen them," says Anne, and we head back to the kitchen.

Back in the kitchen, Anne seems relieved that the guided tour is over. Such formalities are not her style. The house was really never meant to be a showplace. Anne says, "There's nothing formal about a house I have, there couldn't be. It's comfortable, it's casual, and it's lived in." As she talks about her house, Anne's voice never assumes the edge of proud possession. She doesn't rattle off details about this piece or that piece. It's just home.

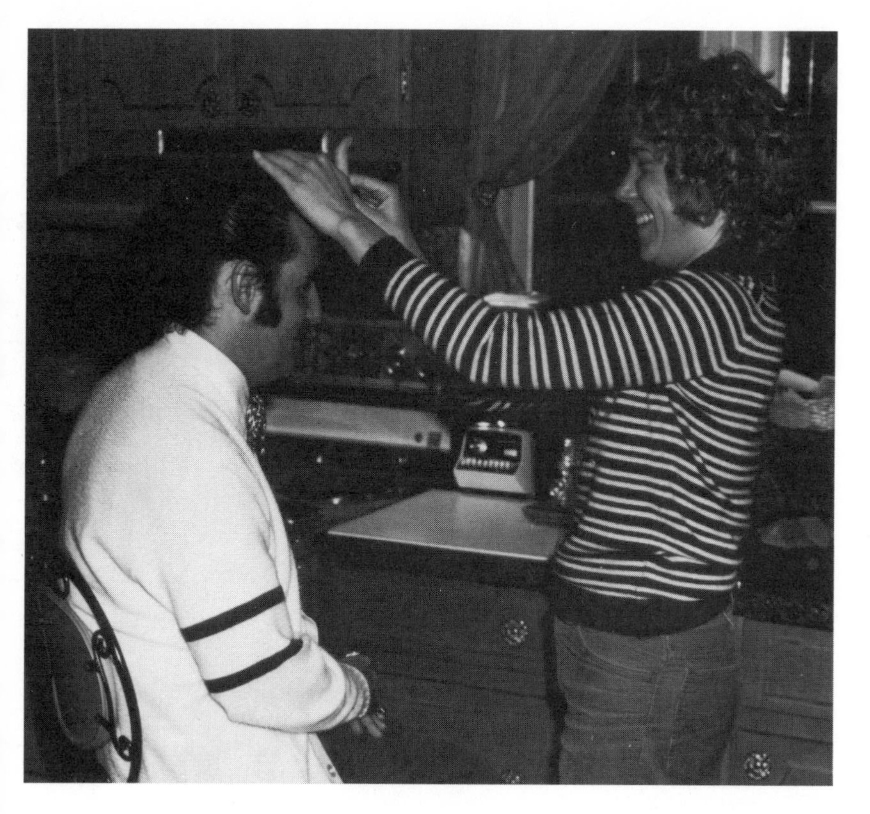

Anne gets Leonard Rambeau ready for a "fifties" party. Practically family (Leonard Rambeau is William's godfather), they enjoy a relationship far beyond that typical between management/client. "People say we're almost like brother and sister," says Rambeau. "There's a mutual trust and respect. I would never ask her to do anything that she wouldn't be comfortable doing."

Even as a child Anne was never one who got a kick out of eating in restaurants. She still prefers home to fancier eateries. Nor is she one for nightclubs or throwing lavish parties. When she has guests, they are likely to be family or friends. Although Rodney Dangerfield may give her a ring when he's in town, or Brian Ahern and his wife Emmylou Harris may drop up when they're around, Anne's two best friends are people she's known since university. One's a fitness expert and the other a teacher. Both live in Montreal. Bill's son and daughter from his first marriage are frequent visitors. In the summer, Bill and Anne holiday at the Murray family cottage in Nova Scotia, and Christmas is another family affair traditionally spent at the homestead in Springhill.

Perfectly ordinary in so many respects, Anne Murray's home life is not completely commonplace. Glancing out the front window on a Friday evening, Anne notices a car stopped in front of the house. "Another goofer," she says with resignation. Bill waves, the headlights come on, and the car moves off. Just another curiosity-seeker hoping to get a peek at the star's kitchen.

nine

A Matter of Taste

AFTER years of seeming to avoid controversial remarks, Anne Murray finally let her tongue fly in April 1981. To the suggestion that after winning sixteen Juno Awards (Canada's rough equivalent to the Grammys) she should exempt herself from the competition and give someone else a break, Anne declared that she had no intention of doing any such thing. In a story in *Billboard*, headlined "Murray Tells Off Canadian Industry," she was quoted as saying, "I don't think it is fair to anyone, including myself, to bow out now and let someone else win just because my name's not on the ballot."

It is unusual for Anne to go around shooting her mouth off. Like her father, she is inclined to say good or nothing at all. That's not to hint, however, that she is not capable of passing strong opinions. She has convictions and favorites and standards. Although she's too famous to walk into a church without causing a stir, "all the beliefs are still there." Her children have been baptized and she plans for them to go to mass regularly.

According to her husband, the one thing that has been a constant buoy to Anne and the people around her is her faith in her voice. No matter how doubt-ridden she was when she faced small crowds in big halls or how many times people told

In 1970 Brian Ahern won a Juno for Best Produced Single, "Snowbird," and Anne won her first as Top Female Vocalist. In April 1981, fifteen Junos later, Anne spoke her mind and declared that she had no intention of withdrawing from the competition.

Opposite. Recording a commercial for the Canadian Imperial Bank of Commerce. After the first year of the campaign, which started in late 1977, research showed that consumer awareness of the bank had increased by fifty-seven per cent.

her she should stand still on stage because "You walk like a football player," Anne knew she could sing. More confidence came with time, and Anne can now say, "I'm relaxing a lot more now than I ever was before. I'm more secure in that I know people know who I am. I don't come onto a soundstage anymore and hear people say, 'Who the hell is she?' " However, she is not complacent. She still knows that it could all end tomorrow.

To make sure that it doesn't, Anne believes in giving the public what they want. "When I choose records, my experience and ears teach me to choose songs that are not only attractive to me but would be attractive to people who listen. Why would you make an album if it was just for you?" At the same time that she challenged the Canadian record industry to nurture other singers that could give her a run for the money in the Juno race, she also let it be known that she found the telecast of the ceremony an embarrassment. The general ineptness of the show (mispronounced names, misread cue cards) got her goat, but what she objected to most were the many in-jokes that meant nothing to the audience at home. "If you deal with the public, you have to try to get to them."

"I've never been one to look into mirrors."

Self-indulgence makes Anne impatient. She thinks the Juno show was self-indulgent, and the same goes for singers, even those she admires, who put their own pleasure first. As she puts it, people like to "relate to a song," and can be put off by fancy gimmickry. "That's the problem I've noticed with some singers. They start way up here and end up down here and have no place to go. You've got to build a song to create excitement. I'm a great one to talk—no one ever calls me an exciting singer, well maybe some people do—but..."

Although not without its quirks, Anne's taste in general is non-elitist. She enjoys golf and watching hockey on television, often taking care of paper work between periods. Her favorite classics are *Jane Eyre* and *Wuthering Heights*, and she enjoys

popular escapist fiction as well. She describes Robert Ludlum's *The Matarese Circle* as "pretty exciting stuff." She also loves movies and, while she doesn't get to go to the cinema that often, she does have a collection of videotapes that includes *The Life of Brian*, *10*, *Same Time, Next Year*, and *Norma Rae*. Her favorite actresses: Maggie Smith, Bette Davis, Suzanne Pleshette, Katherine Hepburn, Greer Garson and Judy Holiday; favorite actors: George C. Scott, Cary Grant, Steve McQueen, Gregory Peck, Spencer Tracy, Laurence Olivier, Alec Guiness, Anthony Hopkins and Richard Burton; and favorite food: lobster, corn on the cob, roast pork and partridge. She once said, "I like almost every kind of music with the exception of acid rock to which I really can't relate,"

"I think when I got into the business and all that, I think Dad was really happy about it, because he saw me doing the things he would like to have done. He was a very successful surgeon — in a small town. I don't think he could bear the thought of being a very successful surgeon in the world."

Opposite. "I could get up for an hour and a half and just sing and say, 'Here's the next song.' But I think it's important to entertain."

Anne throws herself into a soft shoe. "How many of you have ever seen me perform before?...I assume that most of you would not be aware of the fact that I am a really fantastic dancer."

In the summer of 1978, Anne attended a high school reunion in Springhill. "I was probably more nervous going to that reunion than anyone else there. A lot of people assume you've changed because of success. They held a cocktail party in the arena and I can remember stalling, not wanting to go in. But I had to turn the corner and I did. All of a sudden there was a girl I had gone to school with, Cheryl Lee Maine, who came running across the ice. She said, 'Anne!' and threw her arms around me. That was it. All it took was somebody who didn't feel any differently at all."

but, like lots of others of her generation, Anne has gotten out of the habit of listening to new albums, and she still prefers such classics as the Beatles' *Rubber Soul*, James Taylor's *Sweet Baby James*, Carole King's *Tapestry* and the Band's *Music from Big Pink*. Dusty Springfield's *Dusty in Memphis* tops her list of favorites. Like most people with an interest in hit records, she keeps abreast of the music scene by listening to the radio. When she and Bill go on their annual summer vacation in Nova Scotia they are most likely to take along tapes of classical music.

Again in common with many of her generation, Anne has shifted to tamer preferences. She's gone from miniskirts to shirtwaist dresses. She used to drive a fastback Mustang, then a turquoise XR-7 Cougar convertible. Now it's a quiet blue Volvo. Back in her dues-paying years, rum and Coke was her drink. Now she enjoys wine with dinner; from time to time a rye-and-ginger, before retiring. Of course, she still strikes you as somebody who would just as soon crack open a case of beer. As for drugs, in 1973 she told a reporter from a college newspaper, "I've smoked up—I just don't particularly enjoy it, so why bother?" Nowadays it doesn't even seem pertinent to ask her about them.

In one important respect Anne is *not* like her generation, for she herself attaches little importance to matters of taste. Unlike other children of the sixties who became the mass of consumers in the seventies and went crazy over designer labels and serving the latest salad, Anne has a mind of her own. Being hip may serve as a standard to some people but being hip is a concept that Anne Murray has never been able to take seriously.

ten

Anne: The Story Continues...

ON AUGUST 26, 1980, after the opening night of Anne Murray's six-day engagement at the O'Keefe Centre in Toronto (incidentally, the fastest-selling event in the history of the theatre), the Canadian Imperial Bank of Commerce held a reception. On the fifty-sixth floor of the bank's downtown office tower, the surroundings were august, executive suites that looked like a cross between some kind of ancient senate chamber and the mother ship in *Close Encounters*. But it was a convivial gathering, with at least three generous bars, and lots of wives clutching smart summer bags were introduced to friends of their husbands. There were some record company people there; Patrician Anne McKinnon, a former member of the *Singalong Jubilee* cast; a dapper local talk show host with creases in his pants as sharp as teeth; and an outgoing bank executive who thought that a black T-shirt must mean you're with the band.

When Anne Murray walked into the room she attracted an immediate huddle of well-wishers and more wives waiting to be introduced. Surrounded by hot air, Anne was as clear and fresh as rain. Standing back against a wall, out of the fray, was Anne's mother who had come up from Springhill by train

At a press conference held in Toronto in June 1980, reporters were at a loss to come up with questions that haven't been asked of Anne before. "You don't want to hear about my vacation in Nova Scotia?" When a local columnist took the bait, Anne replied, "It rained the first two weeks. That'll make headlines coast-to-coast."

to see her daughter perform live for the first time since Dr. Murray had died. Carefully coiffed, her carriage characteristically erect, she said it was a night Dr. Murray would have enjoyed. Leonard Rambeau also knew it was a special night. Doing it up big in his usual style, he had made sure that the women in Anne's party had corsages to wear.

Anne's good fortune can be traced to the riches of her blood and to the astute judgments of a manager who is also her friend and treats her compassionately. Anne's part of the bargain is a unique voice, unfailing warmth and strength of purpose. Besides that, Anne has star quality. It's true that she's down-to-earth, "not stuck-up," as her fans put it. Just as true, but less frequently noted, is the fact that she radiates. Like any star with sense, she controls her career, but she has a dignity that isolates her from the chicanery of the recording industry. So busy appreciating her lack of pretense, it's easy to overlook things that make her exceptional. She makes conversation

Stepping out at the Stork Club following the Carnegie Hall concert in September 1979.

When Burt Reynolds hosted the Tonight Show *in June 1980, Anne was a guest. Earlier that year as host of* Saturday Night Live *Reynolds introduced her as "the purest, best voice in the world." Although Anne has made jokes on stage about his physical charms, their association is nothing more, or less, than mutual admiration. "I think he's just a wonderful human being. He has time for everybody."*

Anne says of playing Las Vegas that her energy sometimes wanes for the second show, but you'd never guess it from the vigor of her salute.

At Ontario Place, Toronto, 1977. A fan tosses Anne a frisbee. She goes for it.

In the early seventies, Anne ran into a custom goldsmith, named J. Ben Hur, while she was touring with Glen Campbell. Anne had him cast 14-karat bare-foot rings for herself, Bill Langstroth and Leonard Rambeau.

Opposite. In the 1980 year-end Billboard Awards, Anne was named number one adult-contemporary artist.

that is more intelligent than what's average in the entertainment world. She has eyes that enigmatically combine sass and innocence. She says, "If I want to tell someone to go to hell, I will, you know," and most often is heard to utter oaths no stronger than "Judas Priest." She has extraordinarily lovely hands and a salty sense of humor.

Mrs. Murray used to think Anne was an ugly baby. Now she thinks that her daughter is prettier every day. "She only says that," Anne says, "because every day I look more like her." Anne's fans might say that she's a kidder, and Anne attributes her sense of humor to the Maritimes where, even without five brothers to tease you and a mother who thinks you were an ugly baby, people don't let you get away with putting on the dog. Anne in turn has left her mark on the Maritimes. In May 1971 she established a scholarship at the Springhill high school. The Springhill hockey team is called the "Snowbirds." More than that, she has fostered pride in a part of Canada that has been traditionally thought of as deprived.

Canada doesn't really take well to living legends, but in 1978 Anne Murray put out "You Needed Me," a song that even would-be sophisticates had to admit was moving, and went on to achievements that even Canadians had to respect her for. With a tour of Australasia being booked for 1982 (Japan, Hong Kong, New Zealand and Australia), her own American television special, the prospect of her first movie, she continues to break ground.

In 1978 Anne celebrated her first ten years in the recording business. Looking on are Leonard Rambeau and Sam Sniderman, Canada's best-known record retailer.

At a cocktail party following her concert at the London Palladium in April 1981, Anne hobnobbed with the Agent General for Nova Scotia, Mr. Donald M. Smith, and the Canadian High Commissioner, Her Excellency Mrs. Jean Cassellman-Wadds.

And then there are all the cracks she has to put up with about the kind of music she makes. But Anne has become used to magazine writers who start out all smartass and begrudging and wind up saying that she is as nice and wholesome in person as she is on record. Wholesome is too boring a word for the kind of decency that comes with Anne's company. Although in the process of learning never to say never, Anne has made all kinds of contradictory statements about playing Las Vegas or not, doing commercials or not, moving away from Halifax or not, she displays an instinct for the truth. If she has sometimes had changes of mind, she admits them.

Husky-voiced mother of two, strong and lovely and straightforward, Anne Murray is also subtle and fascinating. She has a fortitude that is not visible to the naked eye. Among mere mortals such fortitude is commonly called substance. In show business, they say magic.

Anne at home, August 11, 1981.

Discography

ALBUMS

1968 **What About Me** (Arc AS782)
A: What About Me; Both Sides Now; It's All Over; Some Birds; For Baby; Paths of Victory
B: David's Song; There Goes My Everything; Buffalo in the Park; Last Thing on My Mind; All the Time

"*She sings a folk song well....Anne sings contemporary material well,*" observed Bill Langstroth in the liner notes. Besides songs by Tom Paxton, Joni Mitchell and David Wiffen, there are a couple of tunes with credit to Brian Ahern. Anne herself has never written a song.

1969 **This Way Is My Way** (Capitol ST 6330)
A: Bidin' My Time; Sittin' Back Lovin' You; No One Is to Blame; I Wonder How the Old Folks Are at Home; Sunspots; He May Call
B: Thirsty Boots; Snowbird; Hard As I Try; I'll Be Your Baby Tonight; Nice to Be with You

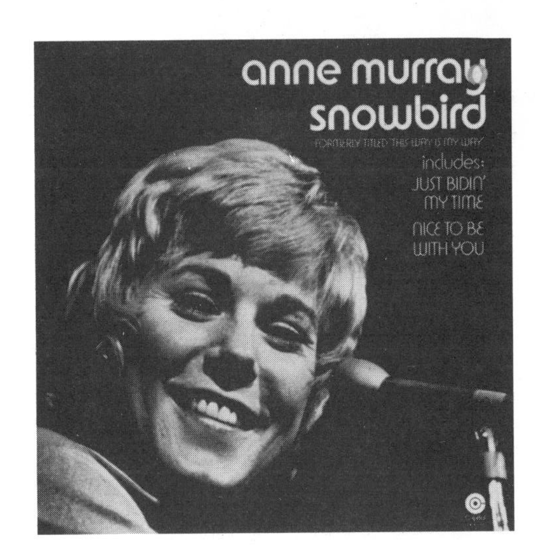

1970 **Honey Wheat & Laughter** (Capitol ST 6350)
A: Fire and Rain; Rain; Someone Else Today; Head above the Water; Break My Mind; The Call
B: Put Your Hand in the Hand; Running; Musical Friends; Get Together; Night Owl

Includes a couple of more songs by Gene MacLellan, a couple by James Taylor. The album title is a phrase taken from "Someone Else Today," a song by Peter Cornell, published by Tessa Publishing, a company owned in part by Brian Ahern.

Snowbird (Capitol ST 579)
Snowbird, released in the United States, was a compilation of *This Way Is My Way* and *Honey, Wheat & Laughter*.

1971 **Anne Murray** (Capitol ST 667)
Released in the United States, this album was made up of tracks from the Canadian release, *Straight, Clean and Simple*.

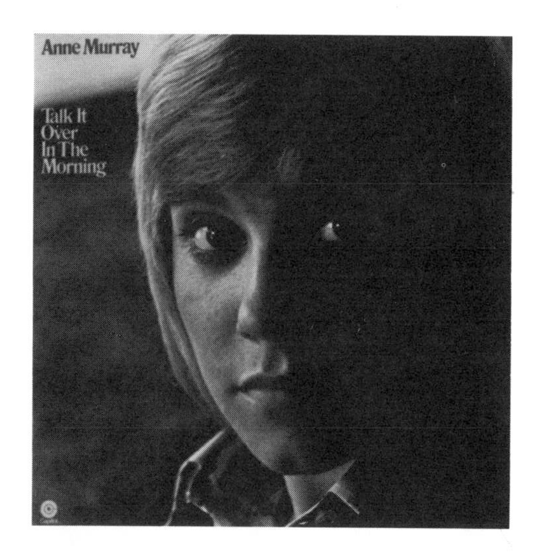

Straight, Clean and Simple (Capitol ST 6359)
A: It Takes Time; People's Park; One Day I Walk; Child of Mine; Sycamore Slick
B: Wishing Smiles Made It All True; Sing High, Sing Low; Days of the Looking Glass; A Stranger in My Place; I'll Never Fall in Love Again

Includes an impromptu intro to "Sycamore Slick," during which Anne breaks up laughing.

Talk It Over in the Morning (Capitol ST 6366/ST 821*)
A: Talk It Over in the Morning; Most of All; Bring Back the Love; Let Me Be the One; Night Owl
B: Destiny; Please Smile; I Know; You've Got a Friend; Cotton Jenny

On the back cover, liner notes read, "*Anne Murray is the kind of girl-next-door who makes you wish the door she lived next door to was yours*."

Anne Murray/Glen Campbell (Capitol SN11992/SW 869*)
A: You're Easy to Love; Medley: I Say a Little Prayer, By the Time I Get to Phoenix; We All Pull the Load; Canadian Sunset; Bring Back the Love
B: United We Stand; Love Story (You & Me); Ease Your Pain; Let Me Be the One; My Ecstasy

1972 **Annie** (Capitol ST6376/ST 11024*)
A: Robbie's Song for Jesus: Falling Into Rhyme; I Like Your Music; Everything Has Got to Be Free; Drown Me
B: You Can't Have a Hand on Me; You Made My Life a Song; You Can't Go Back; Beautiful; Everything's Been Changed

Of her own albums this remains Anne's favorite.

1973 **Danny's Song** (Capitol ST 6393/ST 11172*)
A: Danny's Song; Killing Me Softly with His Song; He Thinks I Still Care; Let Sunshine Have Its Day; I'll Be Home
B: What About Me; I Know; Ease Your Pain; One Day I Walk; Put Your Hand in the Hand

The second side of this album was recorded live at the National Arts Centre in Ottawa. Joanne Brooks, Dianne's daughter and at one time a regular performer with Rough Trade, also sings back-up.

1974 **Love Song** (Capitol ST 6409/ST 11266*)
A: Love Song/Just One Look/Another Pot o'Tea; Children of My Mind; Real Emotion
B: Watching the River Run; Backstreet Lovin'; Son of a Rotten Gambler; You Won't See Me; Send a Little Love My Way

This album is dedicated to Anne's parents: "*For Marion and Carson: This album, all the albums, and all the Love Songs are really yours. Love, Anne*."

Country (Capitol ST 6425/ST 11324*)
A: He Thinks I Still Care; Cotton Jenny; Break My Mind; A Stranger in My Place; Snowbird
B: Son of a Rotten Gambler; Danny's Song; What About Me; Just Bidin' My Time; Put Your Hand in the Hand
This album is a compilation of previously released material.

Highly Prized Possession (Capitol ST 6428/ST 11354*)
A: Dream Lover; Slow Fall; Lullaby; Saved by the Grace of Your Love; When We Both Had the Time to Love
B: Day Tripper; Lift Your Hearts to the Sun; Uproar; Highly Prized Possession; Please Don't Sell Nova Scotia
Reviewing this album in *Rolling Stone*, Jon Landau wrote: "*In the past she's been classified as middle-of-the-road but the drumming (by Pintii Glan) is too hard, the arrangements too intimate for her to qualify for membership in that dreary genre.*"

1975 **Together** (Capitol ST 11433)
A: If It's All Right with You; Sunday Sunrise; Out on the Road; Part-Time Love; The Call
B: Everything Old Is New Again; Lady Bug; Player in the Band; Blue-Finger Lou; Together

1976 **Keeping In Touch** (Capitol ST 11559)
A: Things; Caress Me Pretty Music; Dancin' All Night Long; Sweet Music Man; Sunday School to Broadway
B: Shine, Lay Me Down; Golden Oldie; A Million More; Carolina Sun
Anne regards "California Sun," written by another gifted Canadian female singer, Colleen Peterson, to be the closest thing to the blues she's ever recorded.

1977 **There's a hippo in my tub** (Capitol ST 6454)
A: Hey Daddy; Stars Are the Windows of Heaven; Animal Crackers; Hi Lili, Hi Lo; Why, Oh, Why
B: Teddy Bears' Picnic; Inchworm; You Are My Sunshine/ Open Up Your Heart; Sleepy Time; Lullabye Medley
This album for children was released in the United States as *Anne Murray Sings for the Sesame Street Generation*. It was produced by Anne's musical director, Pat Riccio Jr. Anne herself receives credit as Associate Producer.

1978 **Let's Keep It That Way** (Capitol ST 11743)
A: Let's Keep It That Way; Walk Right Back; Just to Feel This Love from You; We Don't Make Love Anymore; I Still Wish the Very Best for You
B: You Needed Me; You're a Part of Me; Hold Me Tight; Tennessee Waltz; There's Always a Goodbye
This album was dedicated to Anne's husband; "*This Album is for Bill—Love Anne*." Discussing this album and a new album by

*American release

Dusty Springfield, John Rockwell in the New York *Times* wrote of "*two British Commonwealth women singers*."

1979 **New Kind of Feeling** (Capitol SW 11849)
A: Shadows in the Moonlight; You've Got What It Takes; I Just Fall in Love Again; Take This Heart; Yucatan Cafe
B: For No Reason at All; Rainin' in My Heart; That's Why I Love You; (He Can't Help It If) He's Not You; Heaven Is Here

As with *Let's Keep It That Way*, cover photography is by Bill Langstroth.

I'll Always Love You (Capitol SOO 12012)
A: You've Got Me to Hold on to; I'll Always Love You; Stranger at My Door; Good Old Song; Why Don't You Stick Around
B: Broken Hearted Me; Easy Love; Daydream Believer; Wintery Feeling; Lover's Knot

1980 **A Country Collection** (Capitol ST 12039)
A: Walk Right Back; For No Reason at All; (He Can't Help It If) He's Not You; We Don't Make Love Anymore; Tennessee Waltz
B: Let's Keep It That Way; Wintery Feeling; Do You Think of Me; Just to Feel This Love from You; Heaven Is Here

With the exception of "Do You Think of Me," the material on this album appears on earlier albums. It was dedicated to a *Singalong Jubilee* colleague: "*This album is dedicated to the memory of Fred McKenna who introduced me to country music*."

Somebody's Waiting (Capitol SOO 12064)
A: Lucky Me; You Set My Dreams to Music; What's Forever For; Do You Think of Me?; The French Waltz
B: I'm Happy Just to Dance with You; Moon Over Brooklyn; Nevertheless (I'm in Love with You); Beginning to Feel Like Home; Somebody's Waiting

Some fans regard "Moon Over Brooklyn" as one of the finest of Anne's recorded performances.

Greatest Hits (Capitol SOO 12110)
A: Snowbird; Danny's Song; A Love Song; You Won't See Me; You Needed Me
B: I Just Fall in Love Again; Shadows in the Moonlight; Broken Hearted Me; Daydream Believer; Could I Have This Dance

1981 **Where Do You Go When You Dream** (Capitol SOO 12144)
A: Blessed Are the Believers; It Should Have Been Easy; If a Heart Must Be Broken; Bitter They Are, Harder They Fall/ It's All I Can Do
B: We Don't Have to Hold Out; Another Sleepless Night; Where Do You Go When You Dream; Call Me with the News; Only Love

SINGLES

1969 Thirsty Boots*
1970 Bidin' My Time*
Snowbird
Sing High, Sing Low
1971 Talk It Over in the Morning
A Stranger in My Place
Put Your Hand in the Hand
1972 Cotton Jenny
1973 Danny's Song
What About Me
Send a Little Love My Way
Love Song
1974 You Won't See Me
Just One Look
Day Tripper
He Thinks I Still Care
Son of a Rotten Gambler
1975 Sunday Sunrise
The Call
Uproar
1976 Things
Golden Oldie
1977 Sunday School to Broadway
1978 Walk Right Back
You Needed Me
1979 I Just Fall in Love Again
Shadows in the Moonlight
Broken Hearted Me
Daydream Believer
1980 Lucky Me
I'm Happy Just to Dance with You
Could I Have This Dance
1981 Blessed Are the Believers
We Don't Have to Hold Out
All I Can Do

*Canadian release only

Grammy and Juno Awards

JUNO AWARDS

1970 Top Female Vocalist
Best-produced Single: Brain Ahern, "Snowbird"
Best-produced MOR Album: Brian Ahern, "Honey, Wheat & Laughter"
1971 Female Vocalist of the Year
Best-produced MOR Album: Brian Ahern, "Talk It Over in the Morning"
1972 Female Vocalist of the Year
Best-produced MOR Album: Brian Ahern, "Annie"
1973 Female Vocalist of the Year
Pop Music Album of the Year: "Danny's Song"
1974 Female Artist of the Year
Country Female Artist of the Year
1975 Country Female Artist of the Year
1978 Female Vocalist of the Year
Recording Engineer Ken Friesen: "Let's Keep It That Way"
1979 Female Vocalist of the Year
Country Female Vocalist of the Year
Best-selling Single: "I Just Fall in Love Again"
Best-selling Album: "New Kind of Feeling"
1980 Female Vocalist of the Year
Country Female Vocalist of the Year
Best-selling Single: "Could I Have This Dance"
Best-selling Album: "Greatest Hits"

GRAMMY AWARDS

1974 Best Country Vocal Performance, Female
1978 Best Pop Vocal Performance, Female
1980 Best Country Vocal Performance, Female